Glitter and Be Gay

60 years of gaiety and grief

Tim Hughes

Glitter and Be Gay
60 years of gaiety and grief

© Tim Hughes 2023.

Acknowledgements
I would like to thank Steven Cranfield for his expert assistance in proof reading.
Johnny Clamp, the staff photographer at JEREMY magazine.
And Alan Hughes, my very special friend,
for his book design.

ISBN: 978-1-78222-986-5

For Enrique, William, Robert and Guy,
and all my friends and patients
taken by the plague before their time.

Contents

"Never say no to a sexual opportunity,
nor the chance of a television appearance. "
– Gore Vidal

Preface

**THIS IS THE STOPGAP BOOK. After the runaway
success of 'THE NAKED TUCK SHOP' I started working
on another volume of memoirs but along came COVID 19,
the second pandemic in my life, and creativity seemed to
freeze. A friend suggested I publish a collection of my
journalistic efforts and this is that book, with a selection of
pieces spanning sixty years.**

I WAS LUCKY TO BE ASKED to become an associate editor of
JEREMY in 1969. It was the world's first gay glossy lifestyle
magazine. In 2017 my work on this groundbreaking magazine
was featured in the BBC's celebration series of 50 years of partial
gay legality, PREJUDICE AND PRIDE.

JEREMY was sold by subscription only, because WH Smith
refused to sell anything tainted with gaiety. PRIVATE EYE was
also refused sales by this monopoly newsagent in those times.

We very soon went bust and for a short time I became a
contributor to the infamous Bob Guccione's PENTHOUSE
FORUM magazine. It masqueraded as a serious sex education
publication but sailed as near to porn as you could get away with in the late 1960s.

**"In 1972 I followed my
heart – disasterously as it
turned out – and moved
to New York."**

In 1972 I followed my
heart – disastrously as it
turned out –and moved
to New York. I was offered a position as an adjunct lecturer in
drama at CUNY – the city's 24-campus public university
system. I also directed productions Off-Off-Broadway at LA
MAMA and other fringe theatres and for several years had my
own company, the DOWNTOWN THEATRE PROJECT.

I continued to freelance as a journalist, mostly with gay
material, contributing articles to the alternative press, including
the VILLAGE VOICE, SOHO NEWS and eventually the NEW
YORK NATIVE, the city's major gay bi-weekly newspaper.

Now we come to the first pandemic in my life – the gay

plague, GRID – Gay Related Immune Deficiency, as the NEW YORK TIMES belatedly labelled it at the end of 1982. The NATIVE had reported on the disease that eventually became to be known as HIV/AIDS and its devastating effect on our community right from the moment it first became apparent that something virulent was abroad.

Extracts from METROPOLITAN FAIRYTALES, that temporarily abandoned second memoir, will give the reader some inkling of how the plague took over my life. I moved from being a helpful volunteer while nursing a dying lover, to full-on employment in the industry that had sprung up around this deadly disease.

This book is dedicated to the many people in my life, in those early horrendous years, who will sadly never get to read it. ■

Tim Hughes
Amesbury, 2023

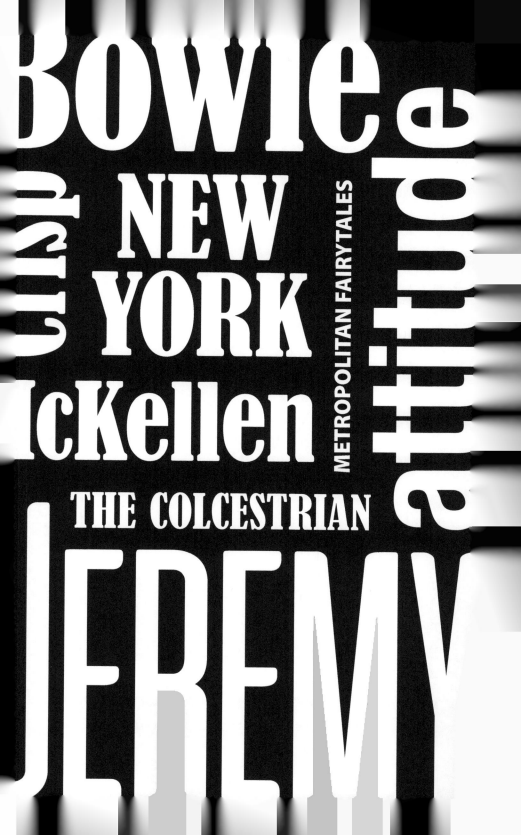

THE
COLCESTRIAN

Vitae corona fides

NUMBER 169 JULY 1962

THE EARLY YEARS
THE COLCESTRIAN
Items from the
school magazine

IN MY LAST YEAR AT SCHOOL, along with my continued desire to be an actor – I had already secured a scholarship place at LAMDA – I won the coveted Livingstone Prize for English Essay. There had been a recent exhibition of rare manuscripts and

memorabilia connected to Marcel Proust and his Venezuelan bombshell boyfriend, the composer Reynaldo Hahn. The essay I wrote about it was probably pretentious in the extreme, even for a seventeen year old lad, but it had given me the opportunity to show my skills at writing my first really long-form piece, as opposed to the short pieces I regularly submitted to our school magazine, *The Colcestrian*. In retrospect, those pieces betray a certain amount of early campery and, less welcome, a somewhat entitled schoolboy snobbishness.

At Speech Day that year in 1962, the prizes were presented by the chairman of the school governors, Dudley Narborough, Bishop of Colchester, whom I wrote about extensively, as being my first gay mentor, in my memoir *The Naked Tuck Shop*. I will never forget the twinkle in his eye, almost a wink in fact, as shaking my hand he presented me with the *Complete Works of Oscar Wilde* – that ultimate patron saint of gaiety.

MASS HYSTERIA?

IT WAS WITH SOME TREPIDATION when I accepted an invitation to the premiere of an American film, that I learned who the so-called star was. The cinema, the Odeon in Leicester Square, was mobbed and I was most surprised to see that a certain Mr Elvis Presley had be-minked admirers. There was a huge cut-out of the star in the foyer, already besmirched by the lip-marks of his many female fanatics. The lipstick shades ranged from 'Hound Dog Blue' to one reminiscent of a new custard product with the enticing name of 'Hot Strawberry'. In the end, perhaps to avoid a near riot, this effigy of worship was snatched away by a member of staff, probably before it was bodily removed by the adoring crowd. In the auditorium eager young faces lit by the reflection from the Technicolor screen were strangely silent. But the audience came near to hysteria, when a young woman, several rows away from me, let out an ecstatic sob and cried, "Elvis, you're a doll!"

1958

CONSTANT HOT WATER

FOR ME THE APPEAL of bath night is twofold – I like to keep clean and I enjoy singing. Our bathroom was in a state of plumbic repair so I decided to give the town's public baths a go. You have no doubt seen the notice outside, *Gentlemen's Slipper Baths*. The slipper reference was rather mystifying but the fact they were for gentlemen made up my mind.

I decided to venture to the baths early in the morning as I did not relish the idea of facing a firing-squad of questions like, "What an earth are you doing in the High Street with a sponge-bag and a towel?"

Furtively I crept through the backstreets but in my eagerness arrived early before the 8am opening time. Three very professional looking regulars were already in waiting. They seemed quite friendly and filled me in on the hazards of using bathroom number three ('the draught gets you something awful') and number seven ('the plug's awkward, mate'). I thanked them and tried not to look too self conscious as I hid my sponge-bag behind my towel.

The door opened and a man smoking a distinctly damp cigarette and wearing a T-shirt that proclaimed the name of the council baths allocated us a bathroom each. Mine was fortuitously number four. The bath and room were spotless. I caught sight of a big, brand new bar of carbolic soap and thanked my lucky stars I had brought my own – Camay, the 'exclusive nine guineas an ounce' variety. I also saw, and rejected, a giant scrubbing brush. I turned on the taps and when it was full stepped gingerly into the bath. All preconceived fears vanished as the welcome warmth seeped through my backside and limbs. The occupant next door in bathroom five launched into a selection from *My Fair Lady* and I managed to catch him up with 'On the Street Where You Live'.

1961

GARDEN PARTY SOCIETY

ALTHOUGH IT SURPRISED ME AT FIRST, I find, on reflection, that the fact that really sophisticated roses do smoke is actually not so surprising.

I remember one evening last summer when the Marigolds were holding another coming-out ball. All floral society was there.

The Marguerites in their positively Ascot fashion told me their Albany houses were being redecorated.

Even the Geraniums at the suburban end of the garden, of course, were entranced by the delicate baroque music that the Lavender ensemble were playing.

The Carnations smiled archly while contesting their humble cousins the Pinks with their all pervading scent. Meanwhile the Fuchsias blew their noses and the Calceolarias munched crisps.

A slight hush in the chatter announced the late arrival of a very handsome Viola, whose long cigarette-holder was chased with sweet-pea tendrils. The Wisteria sighed, and any flower who was any flower clustered round him, for he had written a best-selling botanical novel, concerning the forbidden love of a Briar rose for a Royal Lily, entitled *The Social Climber*.

The Victorian Yellow Rose-buds nestled shyly in a border. One, however, who was far more lovely than all the rest, aroused the

13

Viola so much that he let his cigarette burn down to the tendrils.

The Rose-bud opened her shimmering petals slightly to show the splendour of her pistil's sogma. But dire misfortune, a money-spider had eaten his wicked way into her heart, and as she opened, her petals fell like satin tears and her sterile pistil wrinkled up. The spider was arrested by the Tulip Police and charged with rose-slaughter but fortunately managed a hasty escape. The usually suave Viola was so distraught that he wilted and died.

But society must not be disturbed by such mundane affairs – the floral show must go on. Having moved the star-crossed lovers to a suitably distant compost heap, the flowers refilled their dew-glasses, the Lavender orchestra struck up once more, the Fuchsias blew their noses again and the Calceolarias went back to their crisps.

1960

NEW YORK: CHRISTMAS 1961

EARLY MORNING AND WE STOOD on deck and waited. Suddenly the ship pierced the sea-mist and there in the distance, fabulous and fantastic, was Manhattan – that familiar movie skyline – a bunch of skyscrapers clenched tightly at the bottom of the island. Homeward-bound Yanks yelped with excitement, and even the most die-hard Brit was hard put not to suppress a gasp of appreciation.

The lanky barren banks of the Hudson did not impress me, and most folk returned to their cabins for last-minute packing. We returned on deck to see a strangely small Statue of Liberty slide by as we moved in beside New Jersey and Staten Island. Perhaps the giant image on the post-cards might have been snapped from a very small boat.

The ship nosed past innumerable piers before we eventually reached the Cunard berth at Pier 92 – a somewhat sordid backwater littered with old vegetables and rubbish thrown from the viaduct that swooped above it. It was a far cry from the pristine gleaming Ocean Terminal in Southampton with its generous lounges and hand-waving balconies. We disembarked into a huge draughty warehouse, where my bags were opened, examined, then flung down a chute to be retrieved at the taxi rank. Immigration officers had already interrogated us on board as we approached Manhattan – the stars and other celebrities lined up like us common folk.

The cab driver I chose took me to my hotel opposite Penn Station, so convenient for my trip to Washington, DC by train the next morning.

The traffic seemed no worse than central London but the whistle-blowing windmill cop on point duty seemed rather more exhibitionistic than our own more demure counterparts. I later discovered he had taken the roundabout 'cheat the tourist route' as it was $5 on the meter. I forgot you were obliged to tip and this surly man spat and swore at me as the hotel doorman rescued me and took my bags from the boot. It was the doorman who told me it was actually a fairly quick, approximately five-minute trip, from the Cunard pier – about $1.50 the fare, he said.

My room on the twenty-fifth floor was like all winter weather rooms in the USA – stifling. The windows appeared to be sealed and I was unable to open them. I made a mental note to buy a penknife as soon as possible.

Inevitably, I rushed off to see *that* building – the Empire State one, of course. It was very close by – about three blocks East on 33rd Street. From the gleaming black marble foyer the fastest elevator I had ever ridden in hurtled us to the observation deck. The building seemed to be slightly swaying as I stepped out onto the balcony. Below me stretched the City – endless necklaces of lights, like an entire forest of glowing Christmas trees. My boat, the venerable old Queen Elizabeth, deprived of her regal dignity and dwarfed by the surrounding buildings, twinkled bravely – but convinced no one that she was anything more than a matchstick model. For the second time that day only one adjective applied – the view was utterly fabulous.

Back in my sweaty room I took the penknife I had bought in a shop on 34th Street, carefully slit the window's seals and levered it open. A faint sound of tooting traffic floated up from the canyon below. Around me Manhattan magically seemed to glow and through the wall I heard my neighbour tuning into one of the twelve television channels available to New Yorkers.

1962

Volume 1, Number 6, six shillings.

Jeremy

Stretched out
for you -
our Valentine
and 63
other pages of
gay delights

Jeremy

Jeremy

jer

Volume

What will
your
Fairy Godmother
be giving you
for Christmas

volume 1 number five 6/-

Jeremy

Let's all get together for a gay 1970!

JEREMY

IAN McKELLEN
A STAR IN THE MAKING

IAN McKELLEN IS ON TOUR with the Prospect Theatre
Company's dual productions of *Edward II* and *Richard II*. We met
him in his room in the annex of a rather down market
Southampton hotel. It was necessary to hump a settee into his room
before beginning the interview. Dressed in modish crushed black
velvet trousers and a lilac-coloured grandpa vest Ian lay on his bed.

Why are you playing both Edward and Richard?

"Actually they were never planned to be played together. Toby
Robertson (the artistic director of Prospect) was going to direct
Edward II but he was taken ill. Richard Cottrell, his assistant,
decided to do *Richard II* instead and it was a great success on
tour. When Prospect was invited to the Edinburgh Festival we
decided to do both plays in repertoire. At first it was intended
that I should play Gaveston, Edward's lover, but on re-reading
both plays I could see the two kings were completely different.
So I decided to play both. The consideration was whether it was
physically possible. It has been... but only just about!"

Amazingly Ian plays both on matinee days!

We asked what was the main difference between the two kings?

"Well they don't in any sense illuminate each other. Richard
believes he is a god and his problem is to discover he is a man.
He's rather like a film star I've been working with recently who
has such authority in public that he can't help organizing
everyone's private lives. Edward, on the other hand, is totally
concerned with his private life and finds the business of being
king a nuisance. Richard grows in stature as he becomes more
human, although he deteriorates physically. Edward diminishes
physically but also morally and spiritually."

Which part are you happiest with?

"I think at the moment I am better as Richard – partly

19

because I've already played the part ninety-two times. But Edward is improving – it's much better now than at Edinburgh. Richard is easier. It's a much better play structurally and the character is developed in a straight line. Edward is much bittier – more difficult to develop."

How do you approach a new part?

"It would be nice to come to a part with a blank mind but unfortunately this is not possible with classical plays. These plays are all language and you have to use your voice and body to translate it into a performance."

At this point Ian lit a cigarette. We look surprised as we did not think he smoked. "What I do in private is my own business", he said. This led us to ask about an observation that had been made by Irving Wardle, the theatre critic for *The Observer*: 'It would not surprise me to learn that McKellen has no private life and no need of close friends.' Ian thought that Wardle, who happens to be a friend of his, had only found it safe to say because he knew it was not true. "I think he meant it as a compliment and was meaning he found an intensity in my performances on stage that most people only have in private life."

"If I went to Hollywood and they wanted to know intimate stuff – they would have to make it up."

We asked him when he first decided he wanted to be an actor.

"I was eleven. I did a lot of acting at school and considered myself very experienced by the time I was twelve. Make-up and costumes fascinated me and I had already learned the subtle-art of upstaging the other actors! I was at the Bolton School. We did the usual classical yearly school play but the boys ran a little theatre group themselves – so we did plays all the time. I won a scholarship to St Catherine's College in Cambridge. At the interview they asked me what I was doing. I said I have just played Henry the Fifth at school – so I got in by doing a speech from Henry V! In a way it was my very first audition. They took it away after two years as I was not doing any academic work, just acting with any group who would have me. In my last term I was offered jobs by three different repertory theatres. I took the one at Coventry as it paid seven pounds a week."

What happened next?

"I went to Ipswich Arts Theatre and worked with a brilliant director there called Bob Chetwyn. I played lots of marvellous parts, including Osborne's *Luther*." The following year Ian played Aufidius in Tyrone Gutherie's production of *Corialanus*. It was the opening production at the brand new Nottingham Playhouse. He got rave notices and then did a new play, *A Scent of Flowers*, in the West End. Maggie Smith asked Sir Laurence Olivier to see him. He was soon at the National Theatre in Franco Zefferelli's stunning production of *Much Ado About Nothing*.

We wondered why Ian had left the National Theatre after only one season. "There were too many young actors of the same age vying for the same parts and I wanted to stretch my self working with directors like John Dexter and Bill Gaskill who were also leaving. The National is a wonderfully glorified repertory theatre whose main purpose is to mount classic plays important to the English heritage. Sir Laurence begged me to stay and said, 'he was haunted by the spectre of lost opportunity'!"

At lunch Ian avoided bread and potatoes and drank only one glass of wine. He exercises at a gym two or three times a week to keep fit. We returned to the subject of an actor's private life.

"They don't really have one and work within a prescribed frame – rehearsals, performances and so on. They eat and drink and make love like everyone else. It is not important that people know all the details. All that's interesting about me as a person is my acting. If I went to Hollywood and they wanted to know intimate stuff about me – they would have to make it up." ▪

It is fascinating to re-read this interview over fifty years later. Ian, after many years as a one of Britain's leading stage actors, did go to Hollywood and became a major star. He has become something of a national treasure and is internationally known for his performance as Gandalf in the LORD OF THE RINGS franchise. As for his private life – he has become one of the most public gay entertainers in the world due to his activism around HIV/AIDS and the Thatcher government's anti-gay SECTION 28 in the 1980s. Several times during our interview in 1970 we asked him if he had considered 'coming out'. He said no, never, as it would be the death knell to his career.

INTERVIEW with

QUENTIN CRISP

QUENTIN CRISP has oodles of charm – an almost motherly figure with careful make-up, a blue rinse and a pithy line in witticisms. We met for lunch at the Hungry Horse on Fulham Road, not far from his bedsit flat.

IT IS TWO YEARS since Quentin Crisp's biography *The Naked Civil Servant* was published. Since then he has become a kind of quirky professional spokesperson for all things homosexual. He gets a lot of fan mail but sadly very few phone calls from men suggesting a date.

Despite publicity to the contrary, his book was not a huge success. It sold enough copies to cover his advance with some left over. He told me he is able to manage on a budget of £5 a week and that his main income comes from life modelling at various London art schools. My old friend Denis Wirth-Miller's boyfriend, Richard Chopping, who is a Professor at the Royal College, says Quentin is the most popular life model on the art school circuit because of his sustained stillness.

He has never really had another career. They would not let him join up during the war because at the interview he told them he was queer. The examining board knew he was telling the truth and was not like some of the other recruits just pretending – trying it on to escape conscription.

It is surprising to hear that this gentle soul had experienced so much animosity in his life. He tells me that only last week a man slapped him in the face while he was waiting at a bus stop. "There seems to be an increase in gay bashing – these young skinheads on the rampage. A friend of mine who lives in South London was chased by a gang of them shouting 'pouf' as he was going home by Clapham Common. It was in broad daylight."

Quentin first realised he was homosexual when he was a small child playing charades with two other children. One of them

23

said, "Quentin can play the fairy prince." But the other one opined, "Quentin never plays men's parts." "I remember thinking, Yes, that's right, I never do."

"My mother often encouraged me. I remember when I was about seven her sending me to a fancy dress party dressed as a girl. In some ways she encouraged me to think of my self as a woman. Occasionally she would try and make me pull myself together – but mostly she indulged me."

"My father was completely different – he hardly ever spoke to me. I don't remember ever having a real conversation with him, ever – just questions and answers. But he was never particularly mean to me. I was obviously a disappointment to him – but he never said so and just always paid me no attention."

When Quentin was fourteen he was sent away to boarding school. He was bullied at first because of his perceived femininity. "Do you really have to walk like that?" the boys would say. He hated sport because he was scared of getting hurt and never rode a bike in case he might fall off. "But I learned that if I paid no attention and went on camping around, the boys' all loved it and egged me on to be more outrageous."

His mother never seemed to be concerned about his gayness but as he got older she became more and more concerned about his employability.

"**I never wear drag. I did only once many years ago, just to prove that I could do it.**"

"What are you going to do when you leave school?" she used to ask. "I did not have any skills and I left school without any qualifications. No School Certificates. I did teach tap dancing for a while but mostly I hung out in Soho and modelled. I remember the last thing she said to me before she died was, 'Are you still out of work?'"

"Soho was a very different place to the rest of London in those days – it was run by Greeks and Italians – there was very little prejudice. It was what they called 'bohemian' and you could just be yourself – no one cared if you were gay, or if you were criminal, even. The pubs were a very friendly mix of artists and all of society's outcasts. I used to sit in cafés with my friends drinking endless cups of tea. Soho has become trendy now with all these chi-chi new restaurants and even a few gay clubs that are fully licensed – so perfectly legal."

"I never wear drag. I did only once many years ago, just to prove that I could do it. I dressed up in woman's clothes and caught a bus to the Regent Palace Hotel, off Piccadilly, just past the corner where the rent boys hang out now. I had a couple of drinks with some drag queen friends and then came home on the bus. Absolutely nothing happened – no one even tried to pick me up – it was all quite uneventful. But I had proved I could live as a woman – even if it was just for a few hours."

"I have worn make-up from the time when even eye shadow was considered sinful on a woman..."

"I have worn make-up from the time when even eye shadow was considered sinful on a woman. Do you know that many a young woman had to leave home and go on to the streets so they could simply paint their nails?"

"You couldn't dance with another man then like you can now. Women could dance together even in the big dancehalls – which I always thought was unfair. Something to do with the war when there were no men about, I think."

"There were a few secret places – hidden away in big rooms above shops that were closed at night. You usually went up a back staircase and paid about half-a-crown at the door. The men were either dressed rather formally, or in full drag. It was always supposed to be very secret, but the police knew and would often raid the place. You could be carted off in a Black Maria and kept in a police cell before being taken to Bow Street Magistrates Court the next morning. The 'girls' still wearing their finery, always looked like they had been pulled through a hedge backwards. They would try and defend themselves. But the judge would usually silence them sending them down for six months, no questions asked."

Quentin told me that he had never 'come out' as gay, or identified as a 'tranny'. He thought of himself as just a woman trapped in a man's body. "I never questioned myself about my sexuality, or gender – or any of that gay liberation nonsense. I

just dreamed that I was a woman."

"My flat is full of people at weekends all debating what they ought to do."

"Should they wear their hair up in sweeps – wear pearls – or even have the operation. I warn them that if they have it all chopped off, they will still be no nearer to being a real woman."

We talked about the recent change in the law. [*Editor's Note. In 1967 homosexual relations were made legal between men over 21 but only in private*] "The change in the law makes no difference. You can still get arrested for trying to pick someone up in the street, or in a toilet. Blackmail still happens and there is still a lot of prejudice. People still shout out 'Queer' and 'Pouf' at me when I am walking down the street."

November 1969, *JEREMY Magazine*.

Quentin seemed to welcome a magazine like JEREMY, but with some reservations. He recently told the *Sunday Times*, "Those who are worried about being homosexual may be worried about buying the magazine. But at least it shows them there's somebody else like them. I think if it gives you make-up tips, tells you what to do with the hair on your legs if you wear drag, then it's a good thing. I'm just a freak, an outsider. I can be seen to be a homosexual. You might say I work at it." ■

Some years after this interview I was living in New York and became somewhat friendly with Quentin. He was by then, like myself, a gay transplant from London, and had become very famous after the BBC dramatization of 'The Naked Civil Servant' which starred John Hurt. He was often on TV chat shows and celebrated for his hilarious one-man show, 'An Evening With Quentin Crisp'. We both contributed to the gay weekly newspaper 'The New York Native'. He was their sometime theatre critic and always gave my productions of the 'queer' plays of Carl Morse very good reviews.

Quentin lived in a shabby, sparsely furnished studio apartment on the Lower East Side. Despite his fame he insisted on being in the telephone directory and loved it when complete strangers called him up. He would encourage them to take him out for meals at his favourite local coffee shop. I never remember him offering to pick up the tab whenever I took him there for breakfast. Perhaps this is why when he died in 1999, aged 90, he was found to be worth over a million dollars.

DAVID BOWIE
FOR A SONG

From the Purcell Room to the Palladium – from Zen Buddhism to Art Nouveau, TIM HUGHES and TREVOR RICHARDSON break down the prismatic personality of Britain's New Pop Phenomenon, DAVID BOWIE.

IT'S A BITTERLY COLD December afternoon and David is rehearsing a *Save the Children* charity show at the Palladium. He is going solo with acoustic guitar – wisely dispensing with a bad pit orchestra hastily assembled for this Royal Occasion. Princess Margaret and her chum, Peter Sellers, will be there.

There seems to be a hassle over the sound equipment.

The management seems unable to provide a supplementary mike for his guitar. He's justifiably upset having to make do with just one.

The gigantic white safety drops in behind him. Isolated in a single spotlight against mammoth projections of the Apollo Space shot, David performs his first big hit, *Space Oddity*. It's spectacularly effective and contrasts strongly with the tatty presentation of the rest of the show.

Afterwards David sits quietly with us in the stalls as a strapping Radio 1 DJ introduces a pop parade of stunningly mediocre groups and soloists.

He cracks a stream of excruciating gags while occasionally opening his dress-shirt to reveal a revolting rotating roll of stomach flesh.

Dusty Springfield arrives to rehearse in a trim suede trouser suit. She takes control of the rehearsal. Out go the pit orchestra and in come her sixteen session players, sound balancer, backing girls and extra amplifiers. All of us, David included, are suitably impressed by her dazzling professionalism.

Another scene – another place. The brutalist concrete halls of the South Bank's Royal Festival Hall are filling up with concert goers as an electronic A note summons the cultured to an evening's serious entertainment. Half an hour later the serried ranks of the sober-suited may be seen on the Queen Elizabeth Hall's TV monitor gravely grooving to the sonorities of Haydn with the Amadeus quartet.

Who could imagine that next door in the Purcell Room the group *Junior Eyes* are belting out a big sound, warming up for the appearance of David Bowie. The gig is to launch his new LP released by Philips – his first major record label deal. The publicity says simply that it is given by 'David Bowie and Friends'. It is clear that this refers as much to the audience as to the performers.

David is not a pop star in the conventional sense. He is a switched-on, very creative young man. Rightly admired by the discerning for his talent but only known to the Radio 1 masses for his huge hit success, *Space Oddity*.

In the interval the two audiences surge together into the bars for drinks and two separate cultures mingle strangely – the orthodox and the freaked-out. They view each other's appearance, whether bizarre, or commonplace, with mixed feelings, ranging from amused tolerance to mutual mistrust. But both are curiously united by the same artistic experience, whose only expression

"His heroes are rather surprising – George Formby, Nat Jackley, Gracie Fields, Arthur Modley..."

alters with the vagaries of time and taste. Oddly, the Bowie bunch look more baroque than the Haydn mob.

After the interval David at last appears. Perched on a high stool he begins with some quiet reflective songs, accompanying himself with acoustic guitar. Some of the 'friends' join him and the sounds become more dense. Finally *Junior's Eyes* plugs in again and there's suddenly a much harder sound and one can hardly believe that its centre is this slight and almost Pre-Raphaelite looking figure. The range is incredible.

David says of himself, "I've been grown-up far too long. I could never do a whole programme of unrelenting rock and roll, as most groups do."

His creativity needs more than one outlet and he has too much to express for just one medium. Already his background has unusual variety – art school, tenor sax with Ronnie Ross's modern jazz band, mime performances with the extraordinary Lindsay Kemp, poetry and films. Even now he feels he hasn't really begun to tap into all his resources. Mixed media fascinates him and for a time he worked in a trio with a dancer and a folk singer. He has started writing a musical based on the life story of someone whom everyone's Mum and Dad loves."

His heroes are rather surprising – George Formby, Nat Jackley, Gracie Fields, Arthur Modley – until one

"David takes us on a conducted tour of his mansion – ramshackle yet strangely beautiful in its decay."

realises his admiration for the artist as an entertainer. Modern influences are Jacques Brel, Anthony Newley, John Lennon and Tiny Tim.

We are going to visit David at his home. The car breaks down and we arrive too late to take good photos. The house is a huge, monstrous folly of a place in deepest Beckenham. The lights are on. Door open but no sign of David. He has just popped down to the shops for paraffin and meat for the night's stew.

David takes us on a conducted tour of his mansion – ramshackle yet strangely beautiful in its decay. Sweeping staircases. Huge stained-glass windows. Moulded ceilings. Carved and tiled fireplaces. Art Deco lamps. William Morris screens. There is an almost childlike excitement about the way he pounces on each new treasure – it's infectious. It's a long way from his childhood home in working-class Brixton.

"We have only been here a month and we've hardly started yet. There is so much to do and it's the wrong time of the year." David is living with his new American girlfriend, Angie, but she has gone home to her parents for Christmas. We wonder why he doesn't get professional help.

"No it's my first real place of my own and I want to do it by myself. I'm getting someone to do the ceilings. Isn't the garden wonderful? It's full of birds and animals." Later outside in the failing light during the abortive photo session, squirrels leap through the trees and a fox careers across the lawn.

David is a refreshing change from so many of the inarticulate and untalented charlatans currently littering the world of pop. Unlike them he has something to say because he has bothered to think about himself; about what he wants to do and how he should do it. He hasn't come up with any startlingly original philosophy yet, but he differs from the herd in having a rather meditative attitude to work and life.

Kerouac made a deep impression on him at an early age and he was genuinely affected by his recent death. He was a practising Buddhist for some time and the discipline of meditation has made him reflective. His outlook is however tempered by the exigencies of living in a Western capitalist society and he lacks the mindlessness of so many of his contemporaries. "Money is useful and every bloody hippy wants money to do their own non-capitalist thing. Money means I can afford to furnish my new house as I want." He is not being material – just practical.

The same attitude is seen towards relationships. "I am a loner. I don't feel the need for conventional relationships – sexual attraction is on a continuum between the sexes. I was madly in love last year but the gigs got in the way." He does not tell us with whom.

"His outlook is however tempered by the exigencies of living in a Western capitalist society..."

"I am not really part of 'the Scene' – it leaves me cold. The few real friends I have belong to the period before the success of Space Oddity."

"I just do what I have to do – I want to write songs and the best way of having them performed is to do them myself. But being a performer sometimes gets in the way and I look forward to the day when other people will come along and want to use my material."

"I have this Arts Lab here in Beckenham where there is a lot going on. I exercise a tight control over it. I have to, as free expression often means absolute chaos, and in case they need a

32

leader. It is not cliquey like many of these joints. There are hippies and skinheads and nice young people who don't fit in to any category. They jut come along and if they have something to offer they do it."

It's the midnight hour and the taxi drops us somewhere behind Oxford Street. We plunge down a red lit stairwell. This is the Speakeasy – the club for the 'in crowd'. David is doing the late-night spot. Someone takes our coats and we make our way to the bar. The drinks are very expensive.

The lighting is so murky it is almost impossible to make out the features of the person standing next to you. We are dimly aware of the other inhabitants in this Palace for the Top Pop People. A sprinkling of boys in bone-tight velvet pants

> **"I want to write songs and the best way of having them performed is to do them myself."**

held up by redundant broad leather belts, whose heavy ornate buckles force one's eyes to crotch level. Hordes of girls with deader than deadpan faces stand in predatory clusters – these are the notorious groupies – 'the scene's' attendant Furies. Never mind how hideous he really is. Don't be put off by bony bodies, spotty-white skin, or bad breath. Just one prerequisite – if he grooves, sleep with him. Unless they are aiming for group sex of a different kind, many are not going to score tonight. They outnumber the boys four to one. It's just not David's scene.

The disco music stops and a single spotlight stabs its way through layers of a multicoloured light show. It's David's turn. Perched precariously on a platform of two boxes – a luminous elfin face surrounded by an aureole of blond curls. He looks almost vulnerable. He works the room hard. Numbers from the new LP. Jacques Brel. Some bawdy poems by Mason Williams, even Buzz the Fuzz. Throughout the act there is only a spattering of applause. The groupies carry on parading. People keep right on talking. No one seems involved. The reaction is disturbingly muted.

It's all over and David joins us at the bar. The elfin face looks puzzled.

"I can't believe it – the manager says I got a good reception. If

that's what happens when they like you – what happens if they hate you?" A marauding groupie gropes David in the crutch. "Who was it? I ought to get a fee for that..." ∎

January 1970

At the time in 1969 I had no inkling that David was going to be the iconic star he became in the 1970s – one of the most famous and recognisable singers in the world. Then he was a delightful and intelligent and very attractive young man, struggling to make his mark in an overcrowded pop scene full of pretty boys. He had given an interview to the premier pop music magazine, 'New Musical Express', saying "I've been the male equivalent of a dumb blonde for a few years, and I was beginning to despair of people accepting me for my music and not just my being a cute lad." He need not have worried.

His manager at the time, Ken Pitt, impressed by the gay outpourings when Judy Garland overdosed and died on tour in London, approached us at JEREMY magazine with the idea of marketing his new pretty protégé to a burgeoning gay audience. My fellow journalist and best friend, Trevor Richardson, and I, spent the next two months covering all his gigs and generally hanging out with him.

Amusingly, I will always recall the fact that he was kept on a small allowance by Ken and often pleaded poverty. In fact, he once borrowed five pounds from me to pay his share of the bill in an Indian restaurant. It became an off-told tale for me for many years – that David Bowie owed me five pounds and never paid it back.

This interview is always referenced in the many authorised and unauthorised Bowie biographies, as I discovered the first time I found my name in a bio index. When he died in 2016 I was interviewed by my local paper and BBC radio.

THE GENTLE WORLD OF
PATRICK PROCTOR

PATRICK PROCTOR at thirty-three is one of the most original and successful contemporary artists of our time. He is particularly noted for his sensitive use of watercolour and his paintings of young men. He has had numerous exhibitions at the Redfern Gallery and his work is represented in collections throughout the world, including the Tate Gallery. In addition he has designed for the theatre and was a major contributor to Expo 67.

I went to his gorgeous floor-through flat on Manchester Street with magnificent views of Manchester Square and his particular favourite gallery, The Wallace Collection.

The interview was taped and then edited to capture his conversation.

"I WAS BORN IN DUBLIN but I am not sure how long I was there. I have been back again a few times including last year but I don't feel particularly Irish, even though I love it. I change from day to day – sometimes I feel 'Muswell Hillish' – sometimes I'm Russian. People don't talk about a painter being a Londoner in the way in the way the French talk about a painter being Parisian."

"I went to three prep schools before ending up at Highgate School as a boarder. When I was eleven in the Lower School they made me a prefect. Then I moved up to the Senior School but I never held public office again. There was a very nice art master called Kyffin-Williams and he encouraged me to paint but I don't think I ever said to him, 'I am going to be an artist.' I started saying that to people after I left School. I have never been mentioned in the Old Boys' section of the school magazine. I wonder why – probably because I am gay. I think I would be alarmed if I was, I do belong to the Old Boys' Association and paid the life subscription when I left. I got a letter from them a few years ago saying, 'Now you are making such a great success as a painter perhaps...' I feel quite strongly about the school. For instance I remember vividly the face of the boy lying in the next bed to mine. He was very beautiful."

"My life began when I had to do my National Service. I chose the Navy and really enjoyed it. I was happily stationed right here in London at a hotel in Queen's Gate. I spent most of the time studying Russian at London University for them. When I left art school later I thought of going back into the Navy because I had a romantic fantasy of having a show of water colours by Lt. Commander Patrick Proctor."

I studied at the Slade. But I feel very negative about art schools, the Arts Council and even the British Council – the whole system is creaking. It's a complete conveyor belt formula: development as a student, diplomas, prizes, and finally the collectors who patronise them. I don't believe the schools are completely useless if they stimulate ambition."

"Yes I admit I taught at art schools for a time – Maidstone, Camberwell and the Royal College. Did you know you still have to wear a tie in the tutor's dining room at the Royal College. It drained me, actually. It was based on things other than work.

"Did you know you still have to wear a tie in the tutor's dining room at the Royal College."

I think it is a pity that many young painters have to teach to support themselves instead of the freedom to just make art."

"I did once say that today the painter has to be a performer, but I meant it in a derogatory way. It was based on things other than work – publicity gimmicks, or camping around on television for example. I have not seen my performance in *Laughter in the Dark (A film version of Nabokov's novel with Sian Phillips and Nicol Williamson, directed by Tony Richardson)* yet people tell me I behave outrageously in it. But it's not really me – I'm playing a part. It is so easy for the director to impose character by his selection of shots when he is editing. The voice isn't really mine either, because Nicol Williamson dubbed it. No. What I really mean is a

lot of talented painters are neglected because they won't play up to the camera."

"In my opinion most art criticism is hardly worth reading. I look at the *Sunday Times* to see what's on and the colour supplement has photos I like quite often. People are scared to make their own judgement and have to check out the painter's name before looking at the picture. I admit I used to do it myself."

"Yes I have been influenced by some painters – Bacon , Sutherland and Keith Vaughan in particular, but they are only few of my influences. Why have I taken water colour as my chosen medium? There are so many reasons. I am fascinated by colour television – the way in which colour illuminates from behind, and the way in which a person reflects an intense colour near to it. Light also fascinates me."

"I don't think a lot of painters care about light any more. It's why a lot of modern paintings are so one-dimensional and depressingly flat."

"I love the pressure that working in water colours imposes on me. There is no time to hesitate as it dries so quickly – thought and action come together. It is that immediate. I want to see if I can do that in oils one day. Yes, I know it is a very English thing – but I want to be remembered as the best water colourist of my time."

"Painting to commission is like going on parade – taking your talent out for inspection. I've done several portraits, Tommy Steele, Cecil Beaton, Dickie Buckle (ballet critic of the *Sunday Times*) and Michael Fish (my old pal, the boutique owner and designer who invented the kipper tie). *The Evening Standard* asked me to a portrait of Prince Charles. I painted it, but it was the picture they dare not publish. I could not paint him smiling, and I had to work from photos and sketches of the costume and crown he was to wear at his Investiture as Prince of Wales. It was a failure in the sense it wasn't used. Perhaps JEREMY would publish it. (*We could not get the rights so could not publish it.*)"

"I have designed several theatre productions. *Twelfth Night* and *Total Eclipse* quite recently at the Royal Court. I have never been associated with a hit. I think I would like to do the Living Theatre (*infamous at the time for nudity!*) at the London Palladium.

Funny thing is theatre is always late artistically even with social realism. Late, compared to poets and painters – John Bratby's cornflakes packets came along well before Osborne's *Look Back in Anger.*"

"I don't think I am rich. Artists don't really earn very much money. My needs are very primitive – as long as I have enough for food and fuel. I have always thought of myself as poor but now I am beginning to realise how rich some people are."

"In London I never meet people who send me up like I did say ten years ago. Perhaps it might still happen in the suburbs, or in small towns. The skinhead lads are supposed to be anti-gay, attacking gays out trolling. It is fascinating that there is this new category – as I thought the days of violent teenagers were over.

The rockers were always reputed to be gay. I did some pictures of leather boys a few years ago – pictures in a series and one was called 'Rest Room' and had fifty-six separate leather-boys in it. Someone rang up from the *Daily Mail* and said they wanted to do a piece on me as the Rocker Artist. 'Where did you find all those leather queens', he asked. He thought I was a motorbike rocker sitting in the Ace Cafe on the M1 motorway doing pencil studies of all my friends. Honestly I wouldn't know what to do with a leather queen if I even had one!"

"I once said that a painter was lucky if there was even a short period when everything goes right. They must live for that moment. For me – I think it is coming." ∎

Over the years Procter's early fame and promise faded. Despite being gay he married a neighbour from the building he lived in after her husband died in a car crash. A devastating fire caused by a carelessly discarded cigarette destroyed his fabulous flat with many of his possessions and artwork, including the priceless Flower Power Bedroom – visiting artist friends, including Hockney, Kitaj and Bridget Riley had painted an individual flower on the wall. The fire which made him destitute, combined with being frail and in ill health because of his appetite for alcohol and cigarettes, probably hastened his early death in 2003 at the age of only 64.

A STAR IS DEAD

The legend that was Judy had been in decline for sometime. Shunned by Hollywood, she had come to London to perform at the 'Talk of the Town'. In June 1969, alone in her Chelsea home, she overdosed again on barbiturates. This time she did not wake up.

SHE HAD BEEN A STAR for thirty years and lasted well. She may not have been everybody's singing cup of tea, but the lady oozed charisma. Judy Garland always admitted that she lived on the adulation of her fans, but once the punters had gone home and there was only the echo of applause left and it had died away, she was alone.

She had staying power and talent to spare. Although it was a career littered with lawsuits, illness, controversy, four broken marriages and suicide attempts, she still packed those punters in.

At the last count, in December last year, she had sung *'Over the Rainbow'* more than 12,000 times – a feat that must have made her eligible for at least a special Tony award. But if you think that had been gruelling for her, you haven't heard the worst. Life for Garland had not been exactly a bowl of roses. She may have been a 'legend' but she was human – a fact that newspaper headlines would never let her forget.

She was born Francis Gumm, in a trunk backstage at the Prince's Theatre, Grand Rapids, Minnesota. Her father, Frank Gumm, was a touring vaudeville vocalist, and her mother accompanied him on the piano. She made her debut, quite unexpectedly at the age of two, when she crawled onto the stage during her parent's act. It was the first but not the last time she would stop the show.

Growing up she joined her two older sisters, Mary Jane and Virginia, in a song and dance act called – by a very unglamorous name – the Gumm Sisters. She once told a gay close friend that folks made wicked jokes about 'gumming' – those who practise oral sex by removing their dentures first. The name was eventually changed to the Glamour Sisters after a programme misprint called them the Glum Sisters.

They neither sang, nor danced particularly well, but Judy managed to wow them at MGM and got a contract at the studio when she was only thirteen. Within a year she was starring in 'The Wizard of Oz'. The camera became her lover and while she was still in her teens she garnered twelve more starring roles.

Life did not run smoothly for Judy and even when she was very young she complained she 'was a jangled bunch of nerves'. It was this that led to a series of firings from concert appearances and film roles. Neither was her love life a bowl of cherries. She made all the wrong choices with men, finding it hard to maintain close and genuine, lasting relationships. Her first three marriages failed – the longest to the producer, Sid Luft. In their divorce proceedings they fought a savage custody battle. Her image took a battering when he told the court she was a drunk and had attempted suicide many times.

The gossip and negative publicity made her fall out of love with Hollywood. Lonely and dejected she decided to move away in 1967. Her house, built round a swimming pool, off Sunset Boulevard, was put up for sale and she made desperate attempts to patch up her career. On top of this she was broke and owed several millions in back taxes to the US government.

"She was born Francis Gumm, in a trunk backstage at the Prince's Theatre, Grand Rapids, Minnesota."

Privately, Judy was really being put through the mill – she genuinely believed that Hollywood hated her.

Eventually she found a buyer for the house. "It was a dreadful place really – early Gloria Swanson", she said. "It needed four Chinese gardeners to look after the tropical plants alone. I ask you, who needs four Chinese gardeners?" She was not sad to leave.

Luckily, she landed a major screen role – the ageing musical comedy star in the film version of the Jacqueline Susanne blockbuster, Valley of the Dolls. A pill popping morality tale, it sounded strangely apt – a tale of three women struggling with barbiturate addiction as they climb the showbiz ladder. So things were looking up and then disaster struck. She was fired and the part was recast with Susan Haywood. The studio said she was unreliable, was late too often and left shooting too early.

In fact she said she had found the role difficult – a rude, coarse woman, far removed from Garland's personality. Her only comment on the firing was: "I know I am not in Kansas with Dorothy any more on the way to Oz, but I am definitely not vulgar. I was brought up to be nice and polite."

So she left the silver screen and returned to the concerts again, winning back a fickle public who at that time had pegged her as just another fading movie star. Judy pulled out all the stops and filled the concert dates with all her old

"I know I am not in Kansas with Dorothy anymore on the way to Oz, but I am definitely not vulgar."

hits and the fans kept crying out for more. They really did not mind if they were kept waiting if she arrived an hour late. That was part of the Garland legend. And there was always the chance she might have another big breakdown, sobbing centre stage.

Watching her on stage could be the most electrifying experience. There could not have been another artist who had worked out how to be both offensive and endearing at the same time. Yet she was superbly talented and pandered to the whims of her audience, who in turn pandered to hers. She kissed hands and shook them as though she was running for the presidency. Then there were her onstage jokes, usually at her own expense, about drink and drugging. It was this side of Judy that really sent up to perfection her special image as 'a legend'. No one else in showbiz would have got away with it.

One of her favourite stories was that of the two gay guys who were staying out on Long Island when John Kennedy was assassinated. They noticed all the flags in the area being lowered to half mast and not knowing what had happened one of them supposedly said, "Do you think Judy has died."

The years had not been kind. She often looked haggard with her big brown eyes popping out of her face like king-size marbles. Her voice was worn and thinner but she would just admit that she had a special sound. And who would dispute that? How else could she have held an audience of 28,000 on a wet night in the Hollywood Bowl and still have them crying for more!

When she sang she poured out her troubles and that is what attracted her huge gay fan base – life had dealt her a hard hand and it showed. They loved it every time she put her little finger to her generously painted lips, eyes moistening, in one of those well-rehearsed sobs of joy – the likes of which nobody but her could bring off. There was really nobody else to challenge her in the celebratory chief 'fag hag' stakes – save, perhaps, Liz Taylor.

She had several very good gay British friends and in her last weeks in London, while she packed them in at her 'The Talk of the Town' cabaret season, they really looked after her. It was one of the happiest times she'd spent for while, she reportedly said. They took her out to dinners at the Casserole, the fashionable gay-set restaurant in Swinging London's King's Road. However, she was definitely a homebody at heart and loved the comfort of the rented small mews house on Cadogan Lane, in the heart of the fashionable Chelsea area. This is where her fourth husband of only several months, Mickey Deans, found her dead – slumped on the toilet. She had overdosed terminally on barbiturate sleeping pills, that fateful Sunday last June. ■

It was this article for JEREMY *magazine that may have encouraged David Bowie's manager, Ed Pitt, to approach me to do an interview later that year. He had some weird idea that the outpouring of gay grief for Judy's tragic demise could translate into making David, who was relatively unknown at the time, into a similar gay icon!*

THE JEREMY EDITORIALS

JEREMY magazine's editorials look somewhat naïve and preachy in retrospect, focusing as they did on the need for less promiscuity and the encouragement of some kind of gay respectability. The Stonewall effect – the revolutionary event in New York's Greenwich Village in June 1969 that had galvanised gay thinking occurred just before our first issues – had not really taken hold yet in the gay community in the United Kingdom. There were a couple of crusading organizations like the Albany Trust and CHE (the Campaign for Homosexual Equality). But these organizations were a bit tame and polite. The real surge of stringent gay activism arrived with the Gay Liberation Front (GLF) a year later in October of 1970 and that led to the first PRIDE march in the summer of 1971. However JEREMY was the first magazine, or newspaper in the UK, to use the term, GAY POWER. But it took some while for our beloved Blighty's gays to come out of their closets and 'cottages' and demonstrate in the streets.

TOWARDS A NEW GAY ETHIC

What kind of world for us in the Seventies? An increasingly candy-flossed, plastic, depersonalised and synthetic way of living, or a society where we matter for each other? The choice is largely ours.

Most of us are creatures of habit more than we are victims of circumstance, whatever the various prophets of fatalism may say.

The next decade is ours to mould. Everyone desires happiness. Perhaps too many seek it. One of the universal truths buried in most religions and philosophies is that we are only really happy when we forget our need for it.

Living is dangerous. Freedom is dangerous. The young of today rightly need their freedom – but freedom alone is not enough. It needs to be used creatively. Our freedom is ours to use as we wish. So let us use it! Or else our critics of the 'permissive society' (whatever that means – who can permit what is ours by right?) may have a point if they find in this generation a shying away in the name of 'freedom' from all sentimental ties which threaten us with roots and stability.

The much vaunted 'sexual revolution' has some way to go before the irrational fear, guilt and ignorance bedevilling most people's thinking about sex are swept away. Society is still far too ready to punish 'sex for fun'. Will the Pill, homosexual law reform, abortion on demand and VD cures that are prompt and painless bring in the sexual millennium?

"Living is dangerous. Freedom is dangerous. The young of today rightly need their freedom – but freedom alone is not enough."

The real flaw in uninvolved promiscuity, as an exclusive sexual diet, is not that it is wicked, but that it does not bring lasting or deep satisfaction, even at genital level. This is true of the straight world as it is of the gay.

There is nothing more lonely than a disillusioned 'gay' man who has never had real relationships – only brief encounters. Homosexuality is now an openly discussable fact of life in Britain and that is good. Sadly, so much of the discussion is uninformed, prejudiced, or downright malicious. Homosexuality and ethics are seldom linked and if so more often in a negative way. 'Homosexuality is a sin and wrong' – Full Stop. But it was Sigmund Freud who when writing to an American mother about her son said, "Homosexuality is assuredly no advantage in life, but it is nothing to be ashamed of, not a vice, nor degradation and it cannot be classified as an illness."

If Freud is right, it is not what you are, but how you live that counts; if there is vice and degradation in the gay world, it is because there are vicious and degraded people who incidentally also happen to be gay.

Most folk are not vicious, nor degraded, as the authors of *Towards a Quaker View of Sex* said recently, "Homosexual affection is as selfless as heterosexual affection, and therefore we cannot see that it is in some way morally worse." However anyone who is under the delusion that the very limited legal reforms of two years ago – sex will be permitted for males aged 21 and only in private – means that 'anything goes' is living in dreamland.

"Even today local councils oppose giving permission to open adult homosexual social clubs."

Even today local councils oppose giving permission to open adult homosexual social clubs; gay men still lose their jobs on the mere suspicion they might be gay; and the only advice that can be given to a gay young man who has yet to reach his 21st birthday is "DON'T".

It is progress compared to before 1967, and it was not won without a hard fight to liberate gays from the straightjacket of silence and secrecy imposed by a persecutory law. Now we have the first step towards freedom, it should be used in responsible ways to earn our rightful, equal place in society.

WHO HAS BUILT THE GAY GHETTO?

IF THE GREAT BRITISH PUBLIC had its way murderers would be hanged, thieves flogged, hippies forced to conform, West Indians and Pakistanis sent 'home' and 'homos' put away, horsewhipped, or forced to be 'treated'.

One virtue of the present government is its guts at not pandering to the bloodlust of public opinion. But social legislation is not enough – social attitudes are always in need of reform.

Although in certain spheres homosexuals are acceptable, in

general they are still persecuted. For the majority this important aspect of oneself may have to be hidden from parents, employers and even some friends. This aura of secrecy may gives kicks to a few of the 'old guard' ("...it was more exciting when we were illegal"), but for the rest of us it can spell disaster.

We may have got rid of Victorian prudery, now let us do away with that 'era's' need for furtiveness. It has given rise over the years to a closed world whose customs and even language are enjoyed only by those in the know.

Since it is unlikely that the really intolerant will read JEREMY, perhaps those who pride themselves on their fair-mindedness should ask themselves if they are responsible for this state of affairs. Is it right that those who call themselves 'queer' – perhaps implying some peculiarity, or defect,

> **"As Shakespeare said, 'This above all – to thine own self be true.' Do your own thing, Be natural – whatever that means to you."**

should expect to be treated 'just like other people'? Why indeed do they refer to these 'other people' as 'normal' and 'straights' if not because they regard themselves as abnormal and 'bent'?

Let us put an end to all these labels. The purpose of a liberal education enables men to know themselves – but the quest for self-knowledge is a life-long task. Yet the very existence of the 'queer world' suggests that at some stage a definite choice has been made.

Many young people who suspect that they are attracted to members of their own sex suffer agonies imagining they have to hang this label round their neck and that not going down this unwelcome path may remain repressed for life.

We live thankfully in an age where the old shibboleths are fast disappearing so let us liberate ourselves from ALL the conventions, whether of 'normal' society, or of the 'gay' scene.

As Shakespeare said, "This above all – to thine own self be true." Do your own thing. Be natural – whatever that means to you. Go young man, release into a drab world the energy of GAY POWER. ■

WHEN DO BOYS BECOME MEN?

NINETEEN-SEVENTY has arrived and the 'Permissive Sixties' has been shown the door. JEREMY enters the new decade with a commitment to fight for a society in which we are free, not merely permitted to live the lives we choose, as long as no harm is done to others. We are getting bored with having to wait for 'permission' by the self-appointed guardians of public morals. In the Seventies we intend to lead the life we deserve.

One disgraceful example of the limitations of 'permissiveness' is to be found in the law as it stands for males under the age of twenty-one. "Pederasts", our critics will scream, "homosexuals are corrupters of youth as we always knew." But here at JEREMY we are not talking about little boys.

> "Our critics will scream, 'homosexuals are corrupters of youth...' but here at JEREMY we are not talking about little boys."

We meant those young men who have reached the age of majority – old enough to bear arms and die for their country. This year because the age for voting has dropped to 18 they will be able to go to the polling booths and exercise their democratic rights for the first time. Fighters and voters they may be, adults in all respects save one – they are not deemed old enough to make love to someone of their own sex.

Until recently the situation was at least logical if unjust, homosexual practise was against the law for every male, young and old alike. But the passing of the 1967 Sexual Offences Act has created an anomalous situation which demands immediate attention.

The Wolfenden Committee found that a boy's sexual preferences were fairly well determined by the time he was sixteen. They could find no medical, psychological, or social arguments for making the age of consent different for boys from that that applied to girls. (It is very interesting to note that the Labouchere amendment to a previous act in 1885 raised the age

51

of consent for girls from thirteen to sixteen.) But the Committee finally recommended the age of consent for boys to 21 for three reasons:

1. National Service. 2. The Age of Majority. 3. Full-time Education.

These reasons no longer apply. National Service was terminated in 1960 and the age of majority is now eighteen. As for further education – by what law of logic is it considered permissible for a sixth-form girl, or undergraduate, to consent to a sex act with a chosen partner but not for a boy of the same age.

Nor is there anything to be said for the argument that the law exists to protect 'innocent youth'. Innocence is a moral quality which few possess and most lose at a surprisingly early age. Most young men strongly resent this protection for which they never asked. In any case brought before the courts it is automatically assumed that the older person has seduced the younger. Yet it can easily be the reverse and if boys don't know how to say no to something they genuinely don't want – how on earth can they be considered responsible enough to fight for their country and vote?

As it stands older men are in an intensely dangerous situation with younger people – open to blackmail, threats and even the charming practice of 'rolling' by young lads who think they are doing society a good turn by dishing out punishment and helping out the police.

But leaving sordid matters to one side, there is a whole area of real love, affection and responsible mentoring which is currently persecuted by this unfair and illogical state of affairs. It is a fact that few can deny that a boy's first love affair with another boy, or even an older man, can be a thing of great beauty. That it should be sullied by this whole assumption of criminality is a searing condemnation of the misguided values by which our society is governed. ∎

52

PICCADILLY REPORT

Our reporter TIM HUGHES went undercover for three months in the West End to talk to boys who are 'on the game'. Many work part-time for extra cash. High class trade exists but most of his three month time was spent with the 'Dilly Boys' at the lower end of the trade.

VERY FEW BOYS consciously set out to be prostitutes. Usually a chance encounter spells out to them that there is a seemingly easy and possibly lucrative way to earn a living. Most of the boys are working-class with difficult home backgrounds and come from the provinces – particularly Birmingham, Manchester, Liverpool, Newcastle and Glasgow. They drift to London looking for work and because London to them means Piccadilly Circus they unwittingly end up there. A few weeks hanging around the pubs and pinball arcades, a few conversations with the regulars, an offer of a beer from an older man in the pub, and very soon they have slipped onto 'the game'.

Of course, there are also those boys with some provincial hustling experience who deliberately set out for London where they imagine the pickings will be better.

Most of the boys working the West End are between seventeen and twenty-five, although I met a few who were considerably younger. In one instance I met a boy from Peckham in his early teens. He said he was sixteen but then admitted to being fourteen.

"I wait until my Mum has gone to bed – about ten-thirty. Then I get dressed and slip up to the West End. I get home before she gets up to go to work at 5.30. Then I get a few hours sleep. I don't do weekdays much though as it makes me tired at school. Usually I do it more at weekends. Saturday afternoon – that's a good time. I started doing it last year at our local ABC cinema. I used to hang around the toilets and older men would give me five bob to wank them off. Then I met this other boy who told me I would earn much more up the West End."

There are some older 'boys' – up to middle thirties – but in

a business where youth, or at least the semblance of youth is paramount if you wish to 'score' profitably, they are usually very soon forced off that particular market.

Glossary of Rent Slang

Many of the slang words used by rent boys are also used in the non-commercial homosexual world and sometimes by those involved in the drug scene.

Cottage public lavatory
Gay homosexual
Hustler male prostitute
Quickie brief sex act
Rent male prostitute
Rolling extraction of money by threat, violence or theft
Punter client
Steamer client
On the game involved in prostitution
To score to pick up a client
Straight heterosexual
Working the cottages soliciting in public lavatories

WORKING PLACES

Rent boys work in very specific places in the West End. There are three pubs notorious for rent and the boys are available throughout licensing hours. Such is the reputation of one of these pubs, that younger homosexuals who are not 'on the game' tell me they would not be seen dead there. Two more in Earl's Court have their fair share of 'rent' but it is strictly lunchtime trade; as in the evening they are filled to overflowing with homosexuals who are not 'on the game', and obviously the competition would not work in the 'rent boys' favour.

There are two cinemas in Piccadilly – in one, contact takes place in the stalls and in the other the second circle. These are the least expensive seats in each cinema. Again, the afternoons are the favoured time as in the evenings the cinemas are full of 'straight' patrons. There is also a notorious cinema in Victoria. If you want to watch the film you sit on the right side of the central gangway – on the left if you want to pick someone up. The boys use this cinema in the afternoons.

The pinball machine palaces in Soho and on Coventry Street are popular with the younger end of the trade – those boys who are obviously too young to be drinking in a pub. These amusement arcades are also the favourite haunt of small time crooks and the pimps for female prostitutes. It is not surprising that the boys who frequent them often become in involved in crime.

At the railway terminals of Waterloo, Charing Cross and Victoria the boys often make blatant contact in the toilets. Paddington is popular late at night as many of the boys live in the area. All the stations are shunned by the boys during the evening rush hour, as they don't want to waste valuable time 'scoring' off commuters killing a few minutes in the toilets before they catch trains home to the suburbs.

"All they want to do is toss off at the urinals looking at my prick. Then they're off as they are not interested in paying for it. I haven't got the time to give them free thrills," one boy told me.

The most popular non-railway lavatories are all situated within five minutes walk of Piccadilly Circus and there is a very popular one in Leicester Square. Renter's Corner is the name given to the corner at the bottom left hand side of Regent Street facing Eros. The boys stand along the railings at this rather seedy version of Rome's more exotic Spanish Steps.

METHODS OF SCORING

From several weeks of observation I noted that the boys 'score' in two distinct and different ways – methods of picking up are dictated by location and the character of the boys themselves.

The cool approach is the technique favoured by the boy who does not admit to being homosexual. The boy simply stands at the pub bar with a near empty glass, waiting for a prospective client to ask if he wants a drink. After a brief conversation they leave the pub together.

The alternative blatant approach is a flagrantly sexual display in a toilet. The rent boy stands at a urinal stall until a potential client comes to stand next to him. He will then deliberately reveal and manipulate his erect penis, thereby exciting the score. A few mumbled words, or a nod of the head, indicate that that the two should meet outside.

This method is not popular with the majority of rent boys for several reasons. It is dangerous to behave like this in public places, as plain clothes policemen often watch the West End 'cottages'. Also because the initial contact is sexual and not verbal the rent boy may have picked-up someone who is not interested in paying for sex. It is in fact the pick-up method used by 'cottaging' homosexuals not on 'the game'. The vast majority of rent boys told me they only resort to 'cottaging' when they are desperate to earn money quickly.

CLIENTS

The client is called 'a steamer', or 'a punter', by the rent boy and they fall into four main groups:

The Older, or Middle Aged Steamer

These are by far the largest group. Men who because they are elderly, or feel they are unattractive, cannot easily pick up free 'trade'. They are often wealthy and if they like the boy may try to put the relationship on a more permanent basis making him into the proverbial 'kept boy'. Often the boy is referred on to clients within the original client's circle of friends. In fact they often meet their customers at parties given by this group.

The Married Man

This group may not be old, or sexually unattractive, but because they fear the consequences of exposure with a more permanent relationship, they choose to buy 'trade'. The pick-up often takes place in a lavatory at the steamer's commuter terminus. He is unlikely to risk going to a bar that too obviously caters for homosexuals.

The Tourist, or Business Visitor

The visitor comes to London armed with his 'Gay Guide' and makes for the listed gay bars. The guides often omit the fact that sex can cost money, as the rent pubs are often listed together with ordinary gay bars. The tourist, especially it seems Americans, may not be unduly surprised to pay for sex with young lads as they are accustomed to the 'hustler scene' in their own country. Yet actually London has a reputation for more free sex than any other large city in the world.

The Kinky Steamer

The members of this group use unsuspecting rent boys if they find it difficult to contact 'fellow traveller' homosexuals with more bizarre tastes. This excludes the large leather and motor cycle S&M brigade who have a flourishing free scene at a pub in Earls Court and several open air venues in London most evenings of the week.

Most rent boys are wary of going home with a client they think might be sadistic. This is the dangerous end of the trade, where boys are often plied with too much alcohol, or even drugs – although there are boys who get into this scene to make more money.

One boy told me, "I went home with this bloke to his flat. I saw him slip a pill into my drink. But I knew what do as I had seen it at the pictures. When he went to the toilet I switched drinks and he was out like a light in ten minutes. So I 'rolled' him, got out quick."

Another boy, I was told, who went home with the same man was not so lucky. He woke up in the morning in a park with a ripped shirt and severe stud and leather lash marks on his buttocks and back.

VENUES

The boys seldom have anywhere to take the score once the initial pick-up has been made. Many of them have no permanent private place to live, or share with friends. The venue is therefore squarely in the client's court. This may be difficult for the married man, or tourist.

However there are down market hotels in the Victoria or Kings Cross areas where it is possible to rent a room, no questions asked, for a few hours at a time. Sometimes the steamer may have to pay a full night's rent. The boys will often suggest these hotels as then he can keep the key and after the client leaves use the room to sleep that night.

If the client is not willing to spring for a hotel the boy may suggest using a bathroom at a certain hotel close to Piccadilly. This is not particularly popular at the moment. Bonafida residents sometimes found it difficult to take a bath, complained, and so the hotel employed security to patrol the bathrooms regularly.

The boy may suggest going up a dark alley for a cheap 'quickie', but unless the steamer is either stupid, or drunk, he will fear the possibility of being 'rolled'.

TARIFF

I found that some of the boys tended to exaggerate their earning capabilities. Three to five pounds would be average per client for most of them. If a boy is particularly lucky he may score up to three times in one day.

This requires a certain robustness, or the cunning semblance of sexual excitement. "It is difficult to get a hard-on with some of the older steamers. So I try not to 'come-off' before they do. They don't seem to bother about it so much once they've cum."

One boy told me he received twenty pounds from an American. He assumed the man confused the fivers for one pound notes. He said he usually got ten pounds if he stayed all night.

Often the boy has to do very little to earn the money – perhaps just a short session of mutual masturbation. Fellatio is quite a common requirement, but usually the boy insists on being the passive participant. Likewise anal sex with the boy passive and the client active. It is a curious fact that seemingly very masculine boys will mostly play this passive role. This may be linked to the rent boy's code – where to be active is tantamount to admitting one is 'queer', when many of them insist that they are 'straight'.

If the client requires extras, like kinky sex, the boy will insist on a higher rate of pay. Ranging from fetishists who want to dress up the boy or themselves, in female underwear, leather and rubber garments – to the extreme masochist who wants to be spanked, beaten or urinated on. Some times the requests are ludicrously simple – "all he wanted me to do was to undress slowly, like striptease, and smile at him while he wanked himself off".

ROLLING

'Rolling' does not just happen on the rent scene – but it is a method of obtaining money by the more unscrupulous rent boy. It is a hazard open to all homosexuals who go looking for sex in particular public places like parks, or toilets. It can happen in two ways.

Men searching for trade in a park, or on a common, will be approached by the boy who may suggest a 'quickie' there and then, if the place seems safe. The boy may engage in rudimentary sex act – brisk masturbation or fellatio – or he may merely embrace and suggest that to go further would be dodgy in that location. Afterwards the victim will discover his wallet is missing.

The other type of rolling involves boys working in pairs, or groups. One boy acts as bait for the homosexual to make a pass at – then the other boy, or even gang of lads emerge, offer violence and rob the man.

Rolling also occurs in cinema toilets, or public conveniences that are in deserted places, or do not have an attendant.

The term is also used who steal from a 'steamer' in his home. This may be a surreptitious act, or accompanied by threats of blackmail and violence.

There is some evidence of organised groups of rent boys but nothing like the claims made by certain Sunday tabloids. It may be organised in a very loose way but is not exactly 'Big Business'. It is true that politicians and public figures who cannot solicit in public places may seek contacts in the criminal underworld to supply them with rent boys for a fee.

There are examples of ex-rent boys too old to be on the game themselves, Fagin-like, taking a group of youngsters to pimp under their wing in return for protection and a place to live. But usually the boys find they can make much more money freelance.

Lurid stories of boys provided for 'week-end orgies' at the county homes of the rich and famous are largely apocryphal, or made up by Fleet Street.

There have been a series of recent 'scandals' involving members the Guards Regiments on tours of duty in the capital, but these were most always organised by the guardsmen themselves who are often in need of a supplement to their meagre military wages.

The majority of boys I questioned had never heard of organised syndicates.

THE LAW

The rent boys' attitude to the law may be termed as brazen tolerance, for they are aware that there is very little the law can do to stop them. The police are fully aware of the situation and seem content to turn a blind eye and practise a hands-off approach, so long as it takes place in well defined areas. Occasionally as a result of a complaint from a straight member of the public, who has been mistakenly importuned in a public lavatory – or because one of the Sunday tabloids has decided to make its annual foray into Soho's wicked 'neon-lit jungle', only then do the police sweep into obligatory action.

For a few days the more disreputable bars and public toilets go quiet but as soon as the publicity settles it is trade again as usual.

There are no specific laws aimed at preventing male prostitution – just those aimed at homosexual acts in general – plus importuning, public indecency, acts involving minors and pimps living off immoral earnings.

The fact that money changes hands is largely immaterial but the sex act itself can get the boy into trouble.

Curiously age restrictions under the new law that legalised homosexual acts between consenting adults over the age of twenty-one in private, work in the average rent boys' favour.

If the boy is under 21, he merely has to plead he was not consenting, and the steamer, who is almost always older, gets punished. The law relating to 'living off immoral earnings' concerns pimps only and it is extremely difficult to make such charges stick. The rent boy is most vulnerable to the charge of 'importuning' and so must be very careful not to make the first move when offering his wares. Of course, the law does not protect the older rent boy who is over the age of 21.

THE KEPT BOY

At the upper end of the scene is the 'kept boy', who has very little in common with the humbler rent boy – although he may be also working class but has worked his way up the sex trade ladder. The only common denominator is sex exchanged for money, even if it is deposited in a personal bank account.

They are often from a more middle-class background and may even have a public school and university education. Above all he must be beautiful. He will probably not be as young as the average Dilly boy – but usually in his early twenties, often remaining in the business until his late thirties. By this time he will have amassed enough money to retire comfortably and ironically perhaps be looking after his very own kept boy.

Intelligence is usually paramount.

"I usually try and read all the reviews of new plays, films, books, concerts and exhibitions if possible. That way I can talk intelligently to my employer and his friends quite easily and not just be a pretty face."

Because the relationships are much more permanent and he often lives with his patron, he may hold some official position in the household like secretary, or housekeeper. He may stay with one person for a number of years and he may even love that person.

The business transaction is very seldom simply a cash handout. Usually he is content with an allowance for all his personal needs and of course full board and lodgings. The permanent kept boy may benefit considerably when his patron dies. There are even some kept boys at the higher end of the trade who actually have a rota of rich clients – considerable earnings that are often paid directly into their own bank accounts and they may even have their rents paid.

To break into the high class, a boy must be seen in those places and move in the milieu frequented by the rich. There is very little point in frequenting the Soho rent boy hangouts – although a few up market pubs in Chelsea, or Belgravia, might yield a suitable client. Personal introductions, or being passed on at cocktail, or dinner parties, are the soundest route, or if the boy has the initial means, visits to the South of France, Tangiers, and the Bahamas may be rewarding. ▪

PICCADILLY REPORT was originally commissioned for the SUNDAY TIMES weekend magazine by Robert Lacey, one of its editors, who had been a teaching colleague of mine at Tulse Hill School. Robert later became famous as the author of MAJESTY, an authorised biography for the Queen's Silver Jubilee, and many other best seller biographies. He can still be seen as a go-to commentator for events featuring the Royal Family on the BBC and several American TV companies.

It was however spiked by the powers to be at the paper who considered it too racy for its readership. Fortunately Robert, who was also moonlighting as the editor of JEREMY, decided to recycle it for that magazine. The piece caused a stir and opened the door to me to guest presenting several gay related documentary films for Thames Television, the weekday London ITV channel at that time.

PICCADILLY PROFILES

Last month JEREMY MAGAZINE created a sensation with its controversial report on commercial sex. TIM HUGHES interviews three of the boys who gave evidence.

GORDON

GORDON is just 20. Over a year ago he came to London from Birmingham for the weekend. He never went back and now works in the West End as a 'rent boy'.

"I was pissed off with my job back home working in an electrical shop. So I thought I'd look round London one weekend. I knew I was queer but I did not set out to be rent. The first few days I just hung around the pubs in Soho. One evening this bloke offered me a fiver to go home with him. It seemed like an easy way to earn money so I said yes. I've been on the game ever since."

Gordon is not effeminate. He's tall and sturdy looking. His left hand is heavily bandaged and his hair is absurdly blonde against his brown eyebrows and lashes. "I thought I might do better if I built up my muscles and dyed my hair. But I strained my hand lifting weights and I've decided I don't look any better with blond hair. Anyway some of the other 'Dillyboys' laughed at me."

"I share a room in Chiswick with two other boys – they're on the game as well. If I go home the night before, I get up about twelve. If I spend the night with a steamer I usually get turfed out very early 'cos they want to go to work. Then I come up West to this pub. I buy half cider and make it last as long as possible. Funny thing I don't really like drink much – it makes it difficult when you work the pubs but I don't fancy hanging around the cottages like some boys do."

"A lot of the boys just take drinks off the steamers and don't go home with them. I don't make the first move, just stand there minding my own business. Soon a steamer will come over and starts chatting you up. They always ask if you want another drink and I usually say no. I always tell them straight off that I'm rent. Don't think it's fair to let them think they're getting a freebie and then ask for money after."

"At lunchtime they never seem to have anywhere to go. Usually they're businessmen down from the north for a conference, or something. So I may suggest we go to one of the hotels I know in King's Cross. You have to pay the full-rate even if you only use the room for half an hour. Sometimes I keep the key and sleep the night there. It's only fair."

Gordon went to a tough secondary modern in Birmingham. Some of his classmates have ended up in prison, or Borstal. He has never been in trouble with the police. He left school when he was fifteen. He was going to stay another year but got caned, often for nothing, and it turned him off. Gordon worked in shops mostly but never earned more than thirteen pounds a week – now he make much more than that on a good day.

"I joined the army when I was seventeen but they threw me out after a few months. I used to go absent without leave and one morning the sergeant caught me in bed with another lad. They said I was a bad influence on the other lads – but I really loved that boy. It was a good thing 'cos I couldn't afford to buy myself out."

On a successful day Gordon will get picked-up three times – once at lunch-time and twice in the evening. He earns between three and five pounds from his clients. If someone wants him to stay all night he charges seven. He told me that an American once gave him twenty pounds for a mere half-hour.

"Yanks are easiest really – they only seem to want to suck you off and then they often get embarrassed and want you to leave. I never could understand why they call it a blow-job when it's a suck-off!"

"I never go with anyone kinky – even if they offer me a lot. Once I went home with this cunt. I saw him slip a pill into my drink. But I knew what to do as I'd seen it at the pictures – when he went to the toilet I switched the drinks. He was out like a light – so I 'rolled' him and got out quick."

Another boy who went with the same man was not so lucky. He woke up in a park the next morning with a ripped shirt and severe metal stud and leather lash marks on his buttocks and back.

"I know that I could give it up if I wanted to. I'm just waiting for one of them to offer me a permanent position as a chauffeur, or a valet."

I became rather fond of Gordon and let him stay in the flat I shared with my old schoolmate, Brian Ashen, for a few nights. But he let me down and stole a pair of Brian's antique cuff-links. I went looking for him and found him in the White Bear pub, under Piccadilly Tube station. Fortunately he had not sold them and I got them back. A few months later I got a telephone call from him. He was in Wormwood Scrubs Prison. I went to visit him and he told me that someone he had gone home with had accused him of stealing and taken him to the police station. He said the man had planted some jewellery in his coat pocket. He was charged and got a six months sentence. Gordon told me the man's name – he was a well known manager of pop singers who I discovered later had form for this.

ROY

ROY IS EIGHTEEN. He belongs to the new gay scene, whose members wear trendy clothes from Carnaby Street, smoke pot, and haunt the numerous ambi-sextrous discotheques that have blossomed in the past few years. He likes keeping up. In order to do so he needs an adequate income. The somewhat meagre wages he earns at the boutique he works in are not sufficient and so once a week he rents himself out.

"I've been on the scene about a year now, I suppose. I never want to go back to living with my parents in Ipswich – it was such a drag. There was one gay pub – if you can call it gay. Everyone knew everyone else and the trade was just one long daisy chain. If you had sex with one you felt you had been with the whole gay bunch. Up here it's different – you can see fifty new Dolly boys each day!"

"I was very lucky when I came up to town because I soon got this job in the boutique. At the interview the manager obviously fancied me and I played up to him like mad. But then he fancies someone new every day. There's no hang-ups 'cos I'm good at hustling the customers."

Roy has dark brown hair that curls conventionally down to his collar. He is a neat dresser. His face is urban pale but pretty. An everlasting series of late nights is beginning to take its toll. There are tell-tale shadows under his eyes.

"I soon discovered that I wasn't earning enough money to keep up with the scene so I decided to go on the game part-time, so to speak! Every time I need some new shoes, or a shirt, or something, I troll off to the Dilly and score. It's so easy. I suppose my looks help. Most of the boys down there aren't exactly ravers, are they? I don't really like hanging out there and am always jittery in case I see someone I know – but you do score quickly. How much do I charge? Well, I make it a rule not to go for less than a fiver – more if possible – I think I'm worth it. Some of those regular Soho boys who say they're normal (Ha! Ha!) only do hand jobs. At least I deliver the goods."

Roy does not always use the Dilly. He prefers to use certain pubs in the King's Road – like the Markham Arms – but there are certain drawbacks using these comparatively non-commercial-sex gay pubs.

"I suppose the fellahs I score with are more me but you can never be sure they will pay up – can you blame them? There's so much free trade around there anyway. You're more likely to come away with presents – perhaps a ring, or a silk shirt."

Roy shares a flat with his 'affair', who is a boy of the same age. They are both aware that they are unfaithful to each other and accept this in these 'mod' times. However the 'affair' has no idea that Roy's extra-marital activities are strictly commercial.

"Do you know the thing I am really frightened about? Catching the clap and passing it on to Gerry. That would be awful."

HANS

EVERY SUMMER, for the past few years, a young German student arrives at Harwich. Carrying a duffle-bag that contains not much more than a change of underclothes and socks, and wearing a faded blue denim jacket and jeans, he makes his way to London.

"I think London is the only place left in Europe where one can make a really large amount of money quickly selling one's body.

My address book is full of all the people I have met on other trips to England and I stay with one of them until I move onto someone richer."

"How do I meet my clients? It's simple. My first few days in London I am taken to a bar, or a party – sometimes the party is for me. I soon make contacts at the gathering, as rich middle-aged men seem to find German students very attractive. This year I have stayed with men in Belgravia and Marylebone."

At present he is staying with a friend of mine who has a flat in the Middle Temple, on the Embankment. John is a successful barrister and was only too happy to introduce me to his handsome house guest. What John does not know is that Hans occasionally brings clients back to the flat when he is at work.

Hans is a proud young man but not too proud to occasionally take a place with the boys at the humbler end of the trade. He is a handsome, healthy looking standout among many of the boys on the Dilly, who look undernourished, and often rely on 'pep pills'.

"Money is money! If I feel poor, or need a pair of shoes, or a new shirt I go to Piccadilly, or the Soho pubs. The very first time I went I did very well. It was lunchtime and a man from Manchester took me to a hotel in Victoria and gave me six pounds. His requirements were very simple – he just wanted me to touch him. I kept the room key and went back to the pub in the evening and very soon picked up a young businessman. He was Swiss from Geneva and I don't think he realised he could have got it for free in Earl's Court. He paid me seventeen pounds. Would you not say that was a very good fee?"

The men that Hans stays with are often very generous, showering him with gifts – clothes, records and his favourite – expensive art books.

In many ways he is a very undemanding guest, requiring little ongoing entertainment, and preferring to spend his nights out. He may return to sleep during the daytime and sometimes he will disappear for whole days at on end. Hans knows of many places he can score. The popular bar of a celebrated hotel that caters to wealthy American tourists, or businessmen, is particularly good.

"I usually go to this hotel bar at six-thirty – cocktail time. I do not wear my denims, as perhaps, they wouldn't let me in. This year I borrowed a marvellous pale blue suit from a man I know in Baker Street. It matches my eyes and goes well with my blond hair. Of course, I had it cleaned. It is funny but English and American queens seem to like their Germans blond and blue-eyed and I find it very easy to pick them up."

Every October, for the past few years, a young German student leaves Liverpool Street on the Hook of Holland boat train on his way back to his college in Berlin. He is wearing a very trendy expensive suit and carrying two large suitcases. They are full of stylish new clothes, records and lavishly illustrated art books. ■

KNICKERS IN A TWIST

KNICKERS USED TO be a dirty word. The mere mention of them sent folks into embarrassed titters. And audiences on the popular lunchtime radio show *Worker's Playtime* went into helpless convulsions whenever a comic mentioned that garment of the nether regions. Bums and bottoms were also considered rude and off-limits. And as for any other part of the male, or female anatomy, those generally named 'private parts', these were best left to biology books and teachers.

But with the dawning of the 'permissive society' things have loosened-up considerably. Bums are pretty ubiquitous on cinema and TV screens. We have even had a movie exclusively about bottoms – over 300 varieties in fact – and not just in the controversial films of Mr Andy Warhol but from Hollywood studios also. In this age of the mini-skirt knickers are on full and flamboyant view. Even male underwear has come 'out of the closet' and is available in stylish varieties. And about time, too.

Mummy's advice to us as children was always make sure you are wearing clean knickers – just in case we got knocked down in the street and turn up at casualty with dirty drawers. Not something you would like to be seen dead

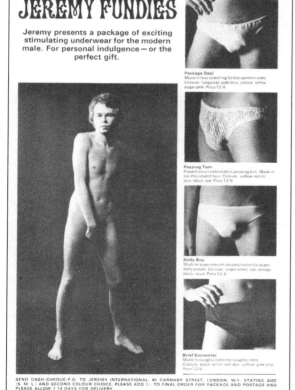
69

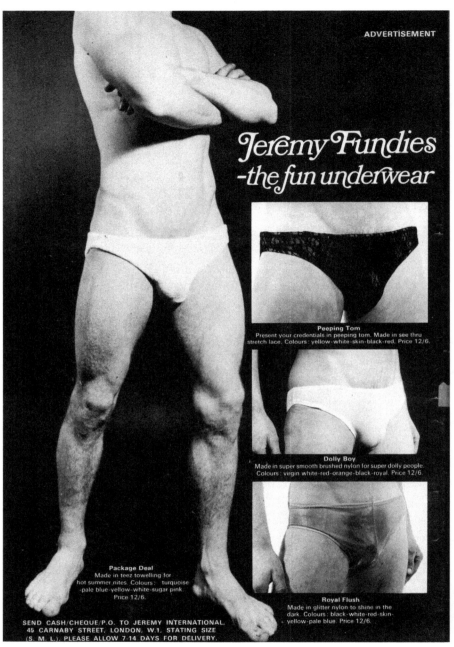

in, as they say.

But perhaps what people really feared was the cruel and off-putting exposure of passion-killer pants. They are scarcely the way to woo friends, or entice the kindness of strangers, when you are trying to win over your new object of affection. In fact many a romance has been stopped in its tracks by the sight of ungainly underwear when one drops anchor, so to speak – in the bedroom or even your favourite trolling spot.

So with trousers being dropped much more in private, or public for that matter, it's not surprising guys have gone overboard for sexy underwear.

Briefs have become briefer and colours and patterns abounds. It's goodbye to the world of Y-fronts. Briefs now come in so many flavours – soft silks, cool cottons and natty nylons. They're the new undercover agents that most modern chaps are proud to be seen in.

Not just available in 'specialist' boutiques, like Vince's, off Carnaby Street, but even Marks and Spencer is leading the way down the path of temptation. So maybe you too can get ahead with a change of knickers.

Don't let passionate breathing be the only thing that comes in short pants. ■

Long before the era of 'budgie smugglers' JEREMY led the way with 'fundies' – a word that I was most proud of inventing. We branded our own line of scanty briefs. Bought in bulk from Paris, we would up the price and then market them via mail order to help raise money to keep our outrageous magazine going and only available by subscription, or from a few very brave independent newsagents, afloat.

I USED TO CONCOCT A GAY HOROSCOPE –
completely phoney with no actual genuine astrology. The idea was to use as much gay slang, and as many double entendres, as possible. Here are some examples.

GEMINI (22 May–21 June)
Friends will be oily this year—
so watch out for slippery
customers. There's no harm in
experimenting a little. After all,
perhaps everything will come
your way.

CANCER (22 June–22 July)
You're becoming over-
exposed, but it's a common
mistake with those born under
this sign. Steer well clear of
rolling landscapes and you
should avoid all bother.

LEO (23 July–23 Aug)
Rather a commercial new year
for you. Decimalisation causes
problems with your rent and
you definitely won't be able to
afford the regular cruise.

72

PISCES (20 Feb–20 Mar)
Its time to pull up your
stockings and get down to
business. Life's a little elastic
now. So dress up, and get out.
You'll be amazed at transformation in yourself.

AQUARIUS (21 Jan–19 Feb)
Be prepared for an active year
ahead. Scout around for awhile
and things will soon slip into
place. However a rash of minor
irritations may occur if you
summer-camp.

SCORPIO (24 Oct–23 Nov)
No need to go far afield this
year. What you're looking for is
probably at the bottom of your
garden. There is no harm in
feeling a little fey occasionally.

LIBRA (24 Sept–23 Oct)
People seem to be putting the
boot in. Being on your uppers
can be soul destroying but
chew things over and you
won't feel quite so down-
trodden and down at heel.

73

GAY SKINHEADS
A BIT OF BOVVER
WITHOUT THE AGGRO

FORGET ABOUT ALL THOSE MODS AND ROCKERS, the NEW LOOK in town is Bovver Boys of the GAY VARIETY. Not the 'gay bashers' that are feared on Clapham Common and Hampstead Heath, but a new breed of likely lads that are guaranteed to get you hot and bovvered in a whole different way.

For starters there is the butch identity that is defined by a manual working-class look in its dress code. Close-cropped hair, or a shaved head, suspenders, or braces holding up artfully bleached Levi 101's, muscle-tight short sleeve Ben Sherman shirts and those signature lace-up Doc Marten's 'bovver boots'.

The 'in' music is Reggae and Blue Beat – energetic and uniform like the dress code – and the dance steps are simple and regular. Not for them the complications of 'progressive pop' and all the with-it stuff of that world – it really 'pisses them off'. You can find them in their favourite lairs: THE DEUCE on D'Arblay Street in Soho, and Tuesday nights only, at THE UNION TAVERN, 146 Camberwell New Road in South London. ■

INTRODUCTION

I WENT TO LIVE IN NEW YORK IN 1972. I had fallen head over heels for a young American I had met in the Coleherne, London's historic gay pub in Earl's Court. He encouraged me to join him after I had completed my London University Institute of Education drama course. It was a disastrous relationship but I loved the post-Stonewall freedom of New York and was determined to stay. I was lucky to find a part-time position as a drama instructor at the City University of New York (CUNY).

The university had twenty-five separate college campuses spread through the City's five boroughs. Tuition was free – a rarity in America at that time – now of course it is fee-paying. As an adjunct lecturer I taught only fourteen hours a week for the princely sum at that time of $23 an hour – of which three hours was running a workshop programme for men incarcerated in the Brooklyn House of Detention.

I had plenty of time to continue the journalistic work I had started with JEREMY magazine and the *Sunday Times* in London. I was living in Brooklyn for the first few years and was able to secure a freelance reporting slot with the local Heights Press. Later I wrote pieces for *Insight, Soho News, New Society* and eventually the *New York Native* – the city's leading gay newspaper at that time. Its relentless coverage of the AIDS crisis from the very beginning in 1981 shamed the regular press long before any coverage in the *New York Times*, or any other US newspaper, except the *Advocate* in Los Angeles – America's oldest gay news magazine founded in 1967. San Francisco and LA were the other cities at the epicentre of the gay plague. ∎

ON THE BROOKLYN CRIME BEAT

I DID A SERIES of pieces on crime in the SRO (single room occupancy) hotels in Brooklyn Heights. These hotels had seen better days and their grandeur – the St. George Hotel once had five ballrooms and two Olympic-size swimming pools – had faded into crime-infested shabbiness. They now catered to transient guests, who were often criminal, mostly involved with drug dealing. There was also a sizeable portion of permanent elderly often room-bound pensioners who were warehoused there by Social Services. It was an unholy and scary mix.

SNITCH PINPOINTS PIERREPONT PERILS

OVER THE PAST YEARS the Pierrepont Hotel has become the home-from-home for a whole group of nefarious ne'er-do-wells. It is populated by pimps, prostitutes, drug dealers and hustlers of every shape. Our reporter, TIM HUGHES, was able to gain the confidence of an informer who verifies tales of the hotel horrors that have spread fear and anger to the law-abiding residents of the hotel and its surrounding neighbourhood.

The informer is part of the hotel crime scene and holds the confidence of the various criminal 'king pins' using the hotel – but seeing an 'out' he has decided to turn informer as the going gets increasingly hot.

Abraham Butnick, the hotel's manager-lessee mentioned in this interview was dispossessed of his position on October 18 and has been replaced by a Mr. Fader, who pledges to rid the hotel of crime. All statements made against individuals by the interviewee are at this time still allegations.

"At the beginning I didn't notice nothing. The bad stuff isn't visible right away. Everything is so uptight – that to a stranger the Pierrepont seems a straight-up normal hotel. After a while I made friends and things opened up. I saw pay-offs but I thought it was small time. Later I joined in and got deeper and deeper. It seemed a cool way to make a living."

"But I will tell you now – if you don't know what you are doing there you could get 'offed'. You must always watch your back. I started informing to the cops when I found they were investigating. Folks in the hotel even have their own snitches to tip them off, you know. Right now I'm after Mr Big. He's into everything – heroin and other stuff. It comes in off the Brooklyn waterfront piers. It's this way – I got to put him away before he rumbles it's me, or I will be in a bad place, man. Or someone will have to come and scrape me off the side-walk."

"Rooms are so easy to rob. Workers in the hotel have keys and get good tips when they open up for you..."

"Rooms are so easy to rob. Workers in the hotel have keys and get good tips when they open up for you. Sometimes they rip off a drunk, or steal an old person's monthly Social Security check. 'Miss Quick' (*the alleged prostitution gay king-pin*) always has a wad of bills from his girl's johns.

"Plenty to keep the staff in extra regular tips. The staff are all definitely in on it, or perhaps they are scared of getting their own heads busted open. They supply pass keys. Sometimes they break up fights and send stabbed folk to the ER at that hospital on Atlantic Avenue. (*We confirmed this with the ER staff at Long Island College Hospital on Atlantic Avenue, at the edge of the Heights*). Anything to keep the 84th Precinct cops out of the loop."

"Why did I become involved? I saw something in it for myself. I'd seen the payoffs done so easy. A guy comes in and puts an envelope, or a package in the flower bin – then a guy comes and picks it up and leaves something there for the first guy. I've also seen the manager, Butnick, pick up an envelope. I hardly ever speak to Butnick so I don't know if he's definitely on the take –

but it looks like it."

"Poor old folk are being robbed and stabbed. But Butnick does not want to be bothered by 'them people'. Only the pimps get the royal treatment when they want something fixed in their rooms. The night before the big fire inspection that the community demanded, a fire inspector guy came to talk to Butnik and he gives the guy an big envelope. Do you think they found any violations? Nah!"

"There is even a Mafia thing going on with the swimming pool in the basement. They turned it into a gay sauna thing called Man's Country. All these fags fucking and using drugs they can buy on site. There are even fags hustling other men down there. It's like that one in Manhattan on West 17 Street called the Everard. That's run by the Mafia and police precinct, you know. (*Note: This is something that was not fully exposed until after the fatal fire where 9 men died, in 1982. When things got too hot the bathhouse moved to West 15th Street in Manhattan.*)

"Look, nothing's gonna change unless you get a whole new set-up. Cops won't clean it up – their harassing just drives it underground. How's a cop gonna arrest a prostitute in her own rented space unless he goes to bed with her and risks getting the clap. They did have a clamp down last summer and arrested a few girls for soliciting. So what happened? The girls all moved over to 4th Avenue to pick-up guys, and then brought them back the hotel. No you need a whole new management here – a complete clean slate." ▪

EXCLUSIVE SCOOP
PIERREPONT PIMP ARRESTED – LOW LIFE EXPOSED

TWO OF THE ALLEGED 'KING PINS' involved with a large prostitution ring centered on the Pierrepont Hotel, 55, Pierrepont Street, have been collared in the last 10 days, according to our police sources.

Leonard Quick, 26, was arrested when one of his alleged prostitutes, a 17-year-old girl, fingered him on a kidnap charge. The charge was eventually reduced to 'promoting prostitution', a misdemeanour in NY State. Quick's auto was impounded, but he has it back now and is believed to have gone across state lines to North Carolina.

The other alleged 'kingpin', whose name was not available at press time, acted as an 'enforcer', or 'strong-arm', in the Quick operation. Both the accused have been living in the Pierrepont for over a year. Surveillance of the crime scene was under the jurisdiction of the 11th Division Detective Squad. Local 84th Precinct patrolmen have made a number of other arrests in the past few weeks.

Francis Ryan, a white female, 21 years old was arrested for menacing behaviour and found to be in possession of drug paraphernalia – hypodermic syringes and needles on September 24th. Two days later on the 26th, Herbert Reese, a black male resident was arrested and charged with rape and unlawful imprisonment of an unnamed female. According to police sources Reese works as a security guard at Brooklyn College, CUNY.

Last Friday, September 28th, two local males locked themselves in a bathroom on the fifth floor (for reasons not yet admitted) and were arrested after they came out. These two defendants, J Ortiz of Jerolemon Street, and L. Johnson of Montague Street are charged with 'Trespassing' and possession of narcotics. ∎

MURDER & DECAY HAUNT ST. GEORGE HOTEL

NOT MANY YEARS ago the Clark Street subway entrance into Brooklyn Heights was a convenient gateway into a special leafy corner of New York City. Driving into the Heights from the Brooklyn Bridge exit, or walking over the bridge from crowded downtown Manhattan, were yet other portals into this charming enclave. Clark Street with its gift shops, corner pharmacy, and its mix of four-and six-storey apartment buildings, crowned by the 'biggest hotel in NY City', was the colourful way into a well-preserved 19th-century brownstone neighbourhood – with the bonus of its grand waterfront esplanade called The Promenade and its sweeping views across the East River to Wall Street and Downtown Manhattan.

IT WAS IN SOME ways a veritable Jane Jacobs kind of block – hotels, apartment buildings, a small commercial strip – pulsing with a 24-hour vitality. Clark Street provided a contrast to the real beauty of the nearby tree lines streets. The convenient newsstand in the subway arcade drew out the raffish characters,

> ## "The convenient newsstand in the subway arcade drew out the raffish characters, like an old New York movie cast..."

like an old New York movie cast – a blonde blowsy woman walking with her poodles, or Pekingese, the bunch of elderly guys debating hot political issues, the bookies, baseball types, and a real live local living movie actor with a gravelly voice holding court.

The St. George Hotel with its fabled five ballrooms, three restaurants and Olympic-size swimming pools, was then the place for an evening swim, a catered affair, a weekend stay for out-of-towners, or a complete room-service comfortable long-time residence.

But now the street has changed. The drug store on the Henry
Street corner, which once offered sit-down counter service, a line
of public telephone booths, along with prescription filling, is
boarded up. The ground floor of the brand new co-op Cadman
Towers building opposite lacks commercial tenants and has
become a dark and dodgy hangout. The arcade has become a
haunt for lurking junkies and other sleazy types.

The St George Hotel itself, which once had a respectable if
shabby gentility in the late 1950s and early 1960s has changed
beyond recognition. It has lost its transient trade in recent years
and has become the setting this summer for three horrific
murders and all manner of other crimes – compounding its

inevitable slide into urban decay and disastrous disintegration of the surrounding precincts.

Two of the murder victims were long-time hotel residents – part of a group of respectable middle-aged, either single or widowed, who had found congenial lodgings, without the excessive space, that kept them free of housekeeping chores. There was still rudimentary maid service and convenient food delivery from the surrounding coffee shops.

The three victims were all attacked in their hotel rooms situated down long empty corridors with many vacant rooms. They were according to the 84th Precinct: Rella Thompson aged 57, found at 9.15am on July 18th with a knife in her abdomen; Joseph Wallace aged 77, found at 8.40am on July 24th with shotgun wounds; and Robert Valestra found at 3am on September 9 in room 554 (where he was visiting a friend) who had been beaten to death. No motive has been established for Mr Wallace but robbery is presumed. Miss Thompson was the victim of a burglary. Further investigations continue but no arrests have been made.

Recently a new social service agency, the Heights Hill Council,

"The agency director, Pat Malloy, tells me that, "The elderly folks here are scared stiff – they talk about the murders and crime all the time."

has taken space in the hotel on the second floor. Community run, its main purpose is to provide advice and assistance to senior citizens in the enjoining communities of Brooklyn Heights and Cobble Hill.

The agency director, Pat Malloy, tells me that, "The elderly folks here are scared stiff – they talk about the murders and crime all the time." Everyone knew the two resident victims. Miss Thompson worked an evening shift in a Manhattan coffee shop so returned to the hotel late. She moved in to live here when things were good. A few people have moved out but though others have talked about leaving they have stayed. Where would they move to? There is crime in all the Heights' five SRO hotels especially the Pierrepont.

There is a definite management problem in a hotel that has a capacity of over 2,000 but that currently houses only 600 – of whom 400 are elderly, mostly living on month-to-month social security checks. The management tells me they are trying to screen potential long term residents.

Most people feel that the perpetrators were non-residents. There is easy access to the hotel from the subway arcade with no security guards. It would be possible for someone looking for dope to walk in from the subway. Go upstairs and mug someone, move on to a different floor to score some drugs and then leave without being seen. It could all be done in fifteen minutes flat.

"Go upstairs and mug someone, move on to a different floor to score some drugs and then leave without being seen."

The rooms for the elderly residents, almost all of which are located in one of three hotel buildings in current use, are on floors which are not completely occupied. A resident maybe surrounded by empty rooms and deserted, scary corridors. The elevators are often out of order meaning one has to use the staircases – unsafe because they're used for drug dealing.

Whole swathes of the huge hotel are empty and semi-derelict, including the once grand function suites and ballrooms.

The Heights Council is planning to operate a Security Table in the lobby manned by volunteer fit Senior Citizens during daylight hours. Working in pairs they would check identification and the room numbers of people entering the hotel. They are just waiting for an OK from the hotel management. It is security on the cheap but it would be a start to increase the safety of the vulnerable elderly residents. ∎

Note: Over time the SRO hotel scene in Brooklyn Heights changed. One reason was the land grab by the Jehovah's Witness sect, who had established their world-wide headquarters on the north side of the Heights. They bought up several of the failing hotels to house their members who staffed the Watchtower offices there. Sections of the St. George were taken over by the New York City's Department of

AIDS Services to house homeless HIV patients in the late 1980s. Many of them had substance abuse issues and this caused unpleasant prejudice in the community fanned by the Murdoch-owned, 'New York Post'.

In 1999 there was a huge fire that destroyed sections of the hotel. Recent years have seen sections of the hotel become student living accommodation for the several colleges in that area and other parts have been turned into luxury apartments.

The Pierrepont, a fine old building dating to 1845, was eventually purchased by a company and converted into swanky apartments. Man's Country, the gay sauna, decamped to West 15th Street in Manhattan in the late 1970s and became renowned for its fantasy atmosphere where patrons could imagine they were starring in a porn movie.

KITTENS ON THE KEYS

STEINWAY TRIES TO RUN a pukka piano factory, but a pack of pussies of the alley cat variety, who have been using the factory at nights for their own catty purposes, has soured the cream.

The stray cats seem to view the handcrafted $50,000 pianos inside the building as nothing more than plush kitty litter trays and scratching posts. So officials at the factory in Queens are doing some caterwauling of their own and setting cat traps.

Factory workers report that they are catching about eight cats a night within the building.

"If the cats use a piano soundboard to relieve themselves, it takes up to six weeks and costs $2,000 to repair the damage."

The kitty capers are a first at the plant, which opened in 1870, and has been the premier piano maker of choice since then. The problem gets worse for Steinway as it sets back production and the slow, painstaking effort that goes into making its world renowned pianos.

The Steinway grand piano – the model favoured by Vladimir Horovitz, Van Cliburn and many other keyboard maestros – takes dozens of craftsman a full year to create. But all their

efforts can be undone in a single night of feline frolics, says Ron, a factory superintendent.

If the cats use a piano soundboard to relieve themselves, it takes up to six weeks and costs $2,000 to repair the damage. He said the company did not have a complete estimate yet on how much the cat invasion has cost it so far.

The cats hide out on the ten acre site until the workers knock off at 4.30pm. When the workers return next morning, they invariably find pianos covered with paw prints, scratches, or worse.

Steinway officials say an illegal garbage dump on the adjacent lot is to blame for the problem. The dump attracts rats, which in turn entices the cats, which use the factory to relax and use as a comfort station after dining.

When the traps snare their furry prey, the workers return the cats to their dump home. But, of course, they are free to have a return engagement the following nights, through the ageing complexes and many nooks and crannies.

The city has been told about the pesky problem and Steinway has even volunteered to clear the dump itself but it has fallen on deaf ears.

A spokesman for the Department of Sanitation said the dead-end street is a classic place for illegal dumping and all the city can do is police the area once or twice a year.

We don't like it, says a spokesman for Steinway. "It's not exactly affecting our manufacturing, but we wish the city would clean it up and put this problem to rest." ∎

SIN, SICKNESS, AND SANITY

AS A CHILD RIDING MY BICYCLE along the winding country lanes of England, or sitting in my grandmother's favourite rocking chair, I little realised that I was indulging in pursuits that might lead me into moral hot water.

Unbeknown to me these were just two of the activities (along with oversleeping, prolonged sitting or standing, straining of memory, overeating and sitting cross-legged) that in the opinion of Victorian medical thought contributed to the 'revolting vice' of masturbation – a practice that could eventually lead to insanity, or even death. The same medical opinion often prescribed that persistent offenders be fitted with gruesome genital devices whose descriptions can only be compared to the various sex toys now available through 'adult toy' mail order catalogues.

Masturbation is just one of the many topics covered in Vern and Bonnie Bullough's 'SIN, SICKNESS AND SANITY', *Garland Publishing*, a fascinating historical examination of sexual attitudes by a husband-and-wife team.

On the subject of husband-and-wife teams I am constantly amazed by the number of authors in marital tandem who litter the field of sexology. Perhaps someone should write a study of this phenomenon.

Masters & Johnson are the most famous example with their clinical probings verging on the almost kinky. But my own favourite couple has always been the couple who co-authoured 'Kiss of the Whip'. In a foreword to the book the couple go to great lengths to express their gratitude to each other 'for years of devoted co-operation'. But I digress.

The authors of the present volume trace the development of sexual attitudes from Greco-Roman times to the present day. We see the various modes of sexual expression pass through gradual stages of re-classification. Initially the early Christian Church lays a stigma on anything more than a strictly procreative approach to sex and so Western Civilization is introduced to guilt and sin.

With the development of medical science in the nineteenth

century the Church begins to lose its monopoly in this area. Anything other than regular heterosexual coupling is re-defined as pathological. Sin has become sickness and guilt is replaced by anxiety.

The influence of the socio-behavioural sciences during more recent decades now forces us to re-adjust our attitudes yet again. Sexual expression ceases to be sick, or sinful, and with certain exceptions – rape, incest, and child molestation – is

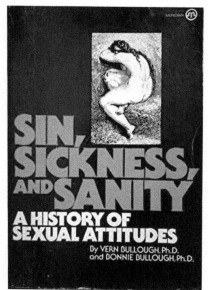

deemed to be healthy and natural – so long as the individual harms no one else in his, or her, pursuit of Eros.

We will all be fairly familiar with the chapter on homosexuality. However, I for one was not familiar with the pronouncements of Messrs. Kellogg and Graham. It seems along with their various inventions of cornflakes and sweet crackers, they also fostered some strange notion that frequent seminal emission via masturbation weakened the male. The resulting degeneracy of mind and body was responsible for – yes you have guessed right – homosexuality.

The authors do not pretend that the battle against the enemies of Eros is won. We still have our Briggs and Anita Bryants to contend with. Rather they suggest that the momentum of the sexual revolution is such that a new society will emerge from the anxiety and guilt hitherto associated with sexuality. It is an optimistic viewpoint and one that depends heavily on more fundamental changes of attitude. But a book like 'SIN, SICKNESS AND SANITY', which examines past attitudes and myths in order to arrive at some healthy understanding of the present, can only hasten this change. ∎

INSIGHT
*– the magazine for
Gay Catholic Opinion*

COMSTOCK COUNTRY

WHAT'S NEW IN PAPUA, NEW GUINEA? It's a long way from Margaret Mead and the Via della Spiga. But that's where last month's Coty Award Winner, Robert Comstock, shot his Fall Collection. A quick shlep down to the Brooklyn Botanical Garden might have been easier, but Comstock believes in doing it the hard way. Real hard. Like finding time to drive the gruelling International Camel Trophy Race across 1,000 miles of rugged mountain, desert and jungle to get there and finish third.

If this doesn't sound like your typical designer – imagine Gianfranco Ferré doing a wheel change – you'd be right. But Comstock is a country boy from Boise, Idaho, fashioning outerwear that's bred-in-the-bone outdoors.

> **"Comstock believes in leather – soft, supple and sensuous like an old friend. 'Leather is so loyal. It's got a longevity you learn to trust... year after year.'"**

Imagine *Deliverance* meets the *SAS*, or *Song of the Loon*, with clothes on, and you've got it. Aficionados of outdoor sports, or other sports for that matter, could swagger in style in these clothes.

We are really in the combat zone here. The outline is definitely macho – there's leather every place. Subtle soft suede and rugged lamb... no, that's not a Middle Eastern restaurant dish. There's jackets – blouson, bomber and fishing; jeans; vests pioneer pants and pullovers all in olive drab and washed out beiges, browns and blacks. Strategic padding and pockets aplenty.

Comstock believes in leather – soft, supple and sensuous like an old friend. "Leather is so loyal. It's got a longevity you learn to trust... year after year."

Comstock knows what he is talking about when it comes to comfort.

You can trust him more than any TV weatherman. Perfect

for our changeable climate – these jackets are mega warm. Cool when it's not, and dry when it's damp.

One secret is in the construction. You can double-up, or single-down on closures and collars. Warm wool knits that zip on, or off, in a trice. There are reversible plaid-lined vests with removable pad pieces, dense enough to shoulder the brutal brunt of any storm. Jackets that sleeve-shed at the jerk of a zip, or the rip of Velcro. But the real secret is in the thermal insulation. 3M, your friend the copy-machine maker, has developed a revolutionary micro fibre more versatile than down. It's lean, light and durable – you control the weather, not the weather you. As the man says, these are clothes for all seasons.

Comstock conquered the Amazon by canoe and tamed the toughest car race in the world. He is fast becoming the top man in the fashion jungle. So there is no reason why New York won't become Comstock Country too. ■

NEW YORK NATIVE 1982

Note. Rather like when I worked at JEREMY magazine in London, a press office, or management company, would approach the NEW YORK NATIVE in an attempt to ingratiate their client with the gay community. The deal was to get them to run an advertisement as well.

BABYLON ON THE HUDSON

SLEAZE AS A STYLE IN ITSELF enjoyed a considerable vogue some years back. It personified people and places that were dodgy and distinctly disreputable – raunchy but FUN. It was like 'dirty talk' for real. Phrases like 'wet and wild' spring to the lips. Sleaze was epitomised by those infamous watering holes like the MINESHAFT and its even funkier little sister, the short lived TOILET. They were all the rage in the late 70s and early 80s – until the arrival of 'the plague' changed gay life for ever. Nowadays sleaze has come to mean something equally disreputable and definitely not fun but squalid – like the lower reaches of current day Christopher Street for instance. It is definitely not a stylish place these days.

Yet there was a time when that particular location with the COCKRING bar on one corner, and BADLANDS on the other, was absolutely spilling over with style. Remember the guy dressed only in a jock-strap, tube socks and construction boots, who used to 'jerk-off' night and day around the corner on Weehawken Street. Or

> **"Sleaze was epitomised by those infamous watering holes like the MINESHAFT and its even funkier little sister, the short lived TOILET."**

remember that vision of absolute style, Rollarena, in her floaty skirt, on skates and waving a fairy wand. Not in anyway a drag queen but the veritable Fairy Godmother of Greenwich Village at night, and weekends at Studio 54. But during the working week he was a former Vietnam Vet who worked as a very straight commodities broker on Wall Street.

Or that long black limo perpetually parked on the corner of Christopher with Washington Street. In the back seat, an ancient man in full evening garb brandishing a champagne bottle and glass who together with a stunning black chauffeur in full uniform, and an attendant female nurse in starched whites dangling a shiny red douche bag from the wound-down window, would offer innocent passers-by an enema and a glass of wine. This was high style in spades.

Nowadays high colonics, save for those souls still fisting, are not really on the menu. Inner cleanliness has given way to outer flawlessness. Witness the shoeshine boy doing brisk business outside the Village Cigar Store at Christopher and Seventh Avenue. The prissy pristine look holds sway as sanitized young men swarm the Village streets, manicured from immaculate head to loafered foot, en route to the new bars off Eighth Avenue and the outer banks of the Upper West Side.

Bars which themselves have gone to the cleaners and are so antiseptic that you

"Nowadays high colonics, save for those souls still fisting, are not really on the menu. Inner cleanliness has given way to outer flawlessness."

could probably eat off their parquet floors – something that would have been distinctly inadvisable in the good old sleazy days. Only that valiant refugee outlaw from the 1970s, the RAWHIDE on Eighth Avenue at 21st Street, remains holding the fort for some semblance of round-the-clock sleaze.

The RAWHIDE attempts to retain that sleazy decadent style with its go-go boys strip-teasing on the bar top. That was the hallmark of the ultimate temple of sleaze in the 70s – the ANVIL. It was the real thing, Weimer Republic-type cabaret but on Acid. It was located at the end of West 14th Street on the lower floor of that infamous hot-sheet hotel of the time, The Liberty, where you could rent a room for sex by the hour. It featured in the notorious 1978 movie, *Cruising*, where Al Pacino, acting as a gay decoy for his NYC police department, is saved in the knick of time from the fate of being fist-fucked.

Street level in the ANVIL was the cabaret – with its fabulous resident 'girl next door' drag act, Ruby Rims, and a host of other performers who did unmentionable things with snakes, or even expelled billiard balls from their rectums in exact time to the music. Felipe Rose who became the Native American Indian in the *Village People* was one of the regular performers.

97

It was so popular that despite a no-entry policy for women – drag queens were allowed – rumours abounded that certain celebrities like Susan Sontag and Fran Leibowitz, and even Jackie Kennedy, would masquerade as 'drag kings' to get in.

Downstairs in a fetid pitch-black basement was the infamous ultimate 'back room'. Sweaty men groped their way through anonymous sexual encounters to the accompaniment of piped disco music while surrounded by several large screens displaying grainy porno movies. All this punctuated by the frequent warning, "Watch your wallets, gentlemen!" Pickpockets were notorious in the dark back-rooms of gay bars and on the dangerous rotting piers at the bottom of Christopher Street where men cruised at night. It was said that the TOILET sex club actually had pickpockets on the payroll.

A few blocks away deep in the Meatpacking District – getting its original name for its slaughterhouses and meat packing businesses – was the MINESHAFT, the most notorious sex club of all time. Its thrill-seeking patrons had to navigate

"Street level in the ANVIL was the cabaret – with its fabulous resident 'girl next door' drag act, Ruby Rims..."

surrounding blocks replete with swinging animal carcasses and workers in bloodied aprons and rubber boots. It was garishly lit – as all the processes of meatpacking in stomach churning view were also in full swing late at nights – and that almost gave it the appearance of a painting by that modern master of sex and violence, Francis Bacon.

If the ANVIL was the kindergarten version of sexual excess, the MINESHAFT was a Ph.D. degree course in kinkism. Located on Washington Street at the corner of Little West 12th Street, it had two floors and roof garden. A steep staircase led up from street level to a large bar area and series of glory hole cubicles, fisting slings and a spot-lit whipping post. A shaft-like staircase led down to street-floor-level dungeon lock-ups, an orgy room, another smaller bar, and a concrete floored area with two unplumbed-in bathtubs for water sports. It was dimly lit and the music tapes featured darker-than-disco pounding music like that of early Kraftwerk.

There was a coat check just inside the door where members could strip down to jockstraps, tube socks and boots. The tube socks were *de rigueur* for a safe keeping place for money and keys. There was a strict dress code for entry rigorously enforced by a doorkeeper – nothing remotely casual, or 'preppie', allowed and definitely no cologne. There was a famous occasion when the celebrated at the time doyen of German cinema, Rainer Werner Fassbinder, was not only refused entry but flung down the stairs for wearing a sweater. However celebrities such as Anthony Perkins, Rock Hudson and a particularly frequent visitor, Rudolf Nureyev, were patrons. A friend reports finding Rudy passed-out on the orgy room floor and fearing that his valuable and probably insured legs might get trampled on, managed to rescue him and take him home by taxi to his apartment building by the Lincoln Center. The doorman apparently seemed nonplussed when he was handed over the dishevelled urine-soaked most famous dancer in the world.

> **"There was a coat check just inside the door where members could strip down to jockstraps, tube socks and boots."**

It was owned and protected at that time, like the majority of after-hours sex clubs and the Everard Baths, by a shadowy consortium of mafia and members of the NYC Police Department on the take. Like a variety of sex clubs, bath houses and gay porno movie houses, in November 1985 it was padlocked by the New York City Health Department. For some time it had been scapegoated by the media – particularly the NY Post and local television stations – as HIV/AIDS took its grim grip on the city. In fact, the vast majority of casualties to 'the plague' had never ever been to the Mineshaft, or any other sex club, and wore preppie clothes. The relentless risk of infection occurring among gay men in the innocent ambience of their own apartment bedrooms practising unprotected sex.

Now in these non-sleazy, un-naughty 1990s, the Mineshaft, or the space where it was located, has turned over a new leaf in the style book. Last time I ventured there a so-called Gay Craft Fair was in full swing. The slings, glory holes and bathtubs had been banished and in their stead a bunch of butch, but politically correct, descendents of the Sapphic Daughters of Bilitis were busy selling folksy homemade sex toys. The ambience was more bazaar than bizarre. There is even an Off-Off Broadway performing space in the former orgy room space and it is rumoured the place will soon be open for Sunday Brunch. ∎

Since I wrote this piece in the middle of the 1990s the area has gone through a glamorous transformation. No longer the gritty slaughter house buildings bustling with nocturnal blood stained and rubber booted meat packers – but now high-end fashion boutiques by the like of Stella McCartney, trendy restaurants, art galleries, and luxury apartments, crammed into a charming cobble streeted expensively gentrified 'on steroids' neighbourhood. In 2009 it reached it's apex of metamorphosis with the opening of a 'park in the air', The High Line Park – the old freight rail line to the dockland piers transformed as a walkway planted with trees and shrubs – and in 2015 the opening of a downtown branch of the Whitney Museum of American Art.

The sleazy clubs and cruisy streets of the immediate post Stonewall Meatpacking nightscape are now a distant memory; rather like the similar decadence and hedonism of the Weimar Republic style cabarets. The sexual freedom that many gay men had longed for had come to a screeching halt and brought with it a devastating pandemic of death.

EXTRACTS from METROPOLITAN FAIRYTALES

THE PLAGUE YEARS

I COUNTED MYSELF LUCKY to be involved with the *New York Native* as an occasional contributor. It had been in existence as an important gay newspaper since 1980 – a year previous to the emergence of the plague. It was in its pages that the rumours of gay men with unusual sickness symptoms became real facts and warned us without a doubt that the plague was already full blown. At a time when hundreds of us were being infected by a virus that was spreading unchecked in bathhouses, gay bar backrooms and indeed our own bedrooms, leading newspapers like the *New York Times* preferred to stay silent and failed to report on a crisis that would eventually engulf our newly gained lifestyle freedoms.

Foremost in the pages of the *Native* were the aggressive 'in your face' articles by Larry Kramer – almost a lone voice at that time. His most seminal and inflammatory piece was spread across the front page of the paper: '1012 AND COUNTING' in the March 14, 1983 issue, and in each succeeding issue for many months he upped the death count. It was the dramatic turning point that finally put the boot into the widespread apathy among a gay community that had seemed loath to give-up the promiscuous lifestyle that was one of the legacies of the post-Stonewall 1970s.

And it was the same Larry, who when he lived in London working for Columbia Pictures in the late 1960s, writing the screenplay for Ken Russell's *Women In Love*, with its sensational

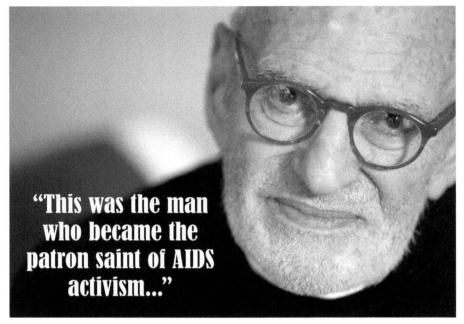

fireplace nude wrestling scene for Oliver Reed and Alan Bates, that had cruised me and picked me up in the supermarket in the Kings Road. I had turned him down when we adjourned for a beer in the Markham Arms pub and did not meet up with him again until I invited him to give a rousing call to arms AIDS lecture at the hospital I worked at in 1990. He did not recognise me but was amused when I reminded him of our own little 'Swinging 60s' moment in London.

This was the man who became the patron saint of AIDS activism and was initially a major irritant for Dr Anthony Faucci and the staff at the United States Centers for Disease Control.

Yes, the same Anthony Faucci who would be in charge of the US response to the Covid pandemic forty years later. One can only imagine how Kramer would have dealt with that bleach drinking-proponent buffoon Trump, if he had not died aged 84 in 2020 in the first months of the new pandemic. But I cannot believe there was anyone more effective in warning of a plague that would soon cause 'a holocaust on the entire world'.

Larry (pictured above) had already, in 1982 – a year earlier to that defining article – one evening in his apartment on lower Fifth Avenue convened a group of friends and instigated the formation of Gay Men's Health Crisis, GMHC, the granddaddy of all HIV agencies, and would go on later to unleash ACT UP, that ultimate engine of AIDS activism. His 1985 play, *The Normal Heat*, based on autobiographical moments in the first years of the plague, would become the defining theatrical record of the early years of AIDS. It had many international productions and was revived again in London and New York in recent years. A film version appeared in 2014.

EL DÍA DE LOS MUERTOS – Febrero 1988

I HAD MAXED OUT MY CREDIT CARD in paying for Enrique's stay in the Clínica Londres – the only hospice-type place in Mexico City that would take persons with AIDS in their final days. In the week before I took him there, a friend had driven me all over that colossal, sprawling city looking for somewhere that could care for him. There was only one free hospital caring for AIDS patients, the government run General

Enrique and me at Peter Rabbit's. Christmas 1983.

Hospital of Mexico, but it only had at that time twelve designated AIDS beds. In New York by contrast by 1988, many of the hospitals were overflowing with HIV cases. Enrique was adamant about not wanting to die in New York but back in his own city and I had promised to take him home.

La Clínica Londres was run by a religious order and so was immaculately clean. Enrique had a room to himself on a very hushed seventh floor with a spectacular view across that vast city to snow-capped Popacatepetl, the mountain that features in Malcolm Lowry's novel, *Under the Volcano.* My skin and bone frail lover lay in his Clínica Londres bed and with a smile told me, "You always promised to take me to London, Timoteo!"

We had been staying in his old artist friend's apartment in the Condesa section. He was also called Enrique, as was their friend and neighbour across the hallway. Enrique's mother, Guadalupe, would make a two-hour bus journey every day, with home-made broths in a big thermos, to look after her son. By that time the opportunistic thrush in his mouth and throat had become so fierce he could no longer swallow whole food and his incontinence was so distressing we had to change the bed linen three, or four times a day. I was exhausted.

He died after three days. The telephone call came at 5am. I felt bad, cursing myself for not staying through the night as I had left him at 11pm. Enrique Hernández arranged a taxi for me and as the sun rose I made the lonely journey across the city to the clinic. Enrique had been washed and was laid out on the bed in a linen shroud. I kissed him on the forehead and sat with his body for a private eternity revisiting all the events in our seven years together – beginning with that fateful telephone call from Tamara.

Tamara Bliss, my old Russian émigré friend with the exotic name right out of a James Bond movie. We had collaborated on productions for many years and I had stayed in her spare room when I was between apartments once. She had composed the music for my Soho Theatre production of *Twelfth Night* in 1975. Tamara taught music history at the New School and also gave private English language lessons.

"I have a new student from Mexico. He is an artist and has just finished designing *Cavalleria Rusticana* and *Pagliacci* for the Arizona Opera Company. He needs New York friends and I know you would like him."

She asked me to come to an early supper the following evening to meet him. I did like him – in fact I fell in love with him on the spot. That same evening Tamara conveniently absented herself to teach a late class at the New School. We had sex in that same spare room. He had been staying in Brooklyn with a friend of Tamara's but the next day he moved in with me on West 10th Street for what I hoped would be for ever.

The clinic absolutely refused to release his body until I paid up and the funeral tradition in Mexico is to have a burial within forty-eight hours. Enrique Hernandez and his other friends were archetypal struggling artists so could not help. His mother, with my help, paid for the funeral. So that is how my credit card came to be maxed.

WHEN I RETURNED from Enrique's funeral in Mexico City it was time for a big life change. His illness, and before that the unrelenting sickness of many of our friends, had consumed the waking hours of my life for almost five years.

Besides caring for Enrique and volunteering with several HIV groups I was working as the part-time editor of DESIGNER REPORT – the bi-monthly publication for a fashion-trending outfit run by my friend, Alvin Bell. The trips to Paris and Milan were fun but the job was not paying the bills. Enrique had eventually become too sick to take on any set design commissions, or continue working at a friend's silk screen studio.

I found work in an HIV/AIDS programme. The plague had created a whole industry of job opportunities and by good fortune I secured a position in the social work department at my local hospital, Beth Israel, five minutes from my apartment in the East Village. It was the first full-time position I had had since I arrived in New York from London in 1972 – having survived for sixteen years on a patchwork portfolio of jobs – teaching drama at the City University (CUNY), occasional theatre directing, counselling at a Planned Parenthood affiliate, and freelance journalism. The salary was decent and the real bonus for anyone working in America – the job came with

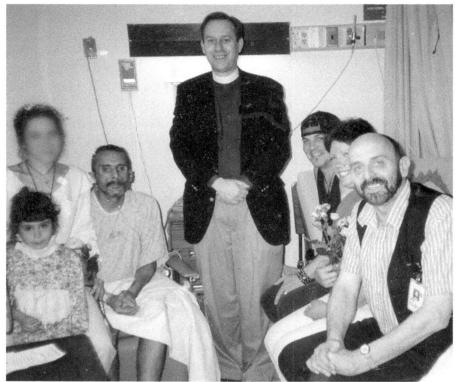
Above: Luis H marries his long term partner – a dying wish.

complete medical and dental insurance.

Beth Israel, a Jewish-founded hospital on the edge of the East Village, along with St Vincent's, its Catholic counterpart in the nearby West Village, had been in the forefront of HIV treatment and care since the very beginning of the plague in 1981. I had my own office in its standalone outpatient facility, the Peter Kreuger Clinic. It had been named and bequeathed by a wealthy family, whose gay young stockbroker son had died in the very early years of the pandemic. Most of the patients were poor and on Medicaid, the government health insurance program that covered their treatment and provided a safety net for the many others who had had to stop working and were forced into poverty by the disease. ∎

IN MEMORIAM

BETH ISRAEL had also gained a reputation for looking after private patients who were also celebrities – Steve Rubell of Studio 54 fame, Tina Chow, the glamorous international model and wife of Restauranteurs, Michael Chow, and my old friend Robert Mapplethorpe (pictured below). Working in the clinic I seldom met these 'celebrity' patients unless a doctor treating them asked for my assistance as a favour. However, many of the persons with HIV/AIDS I had on my case load were celebrated in their own right.

I looked after an amazing variety of young men and women over the ten years I worked in the clinic. The disease had by that time moved beyond gay men and a good number of my patients had contracted the virus through intravenous drug use and a percentage of them were their sexual partners. I even had a

distressingly small group of complete families who were infected – father, mother and their children. Eventually the hospital set-up a brilliant programme to provide special care to these children and their parents. It was run by my very skilful co-worker and friend, Dina Franchi.

Mahindra was an Indian immigrant from Trinidad, who I had met before when he was the assistant manager at my branch of Citi Bank. His mother came to New York to care for him in his last months and insisted on making and bringing to the clinic my favourite dishes when she learned I loved Indian food.

Juan was from East Harlem. As a teenager he had been for a time a champion light-weight boxer. He was in the closet, and even went so far as to cover-up the reason for his infection by telling friends and family he had injected heroin.

There was a delightful Vietnamese patient, Lan, whose back story was almost the gay version of *Miss Saigon*. As a young teenager he had a relationship with a US Army officer who rescued him at the end of the war and brought him to America. Sadly his rescuer in true *Butterfly* style deserted Lan as he grew older. But he managed to put himself through college and become a teacher – eventually getting a lectureship at NYU.

I had a string of Cuban patients who had either escaped from Cuba, or had been part of the Mariel boat lift in 1980, when the Castro government deported a large number of criminals and in their words 'degenerates' – in other words gays – to Florida. It was suggested by some homophobic conspiracy theorists that these 'Marelitos' were responsible for bringing HIV to America as Castro had deployed soldiers to Africa to assist the Angolan Communists. It was true that HIV was believed to have jumped species in Africa – but the timeline of the disease in the United States made these accusations more than dubious.

There was extraordinary help given to some of my patients by actual celebrities. I had a patient, Roberto, whose parents were the caretakers of the synagogue on Fifth Avenue where the comedian Joan Rivers worshipped. Roberto walked her dog and she stepped in to support him financially when he could no longer work. And Madonna, without an ounce of publicity, even paid the bills and rents for a whole group of my Latino patients – young men that she had known and worked with before she became a star, when she was a dance student working as the 'coat check girl' at the club, Dancetaria, the celebrated alternative to Studio 54. ∎

10th Street Gallery: ENRIQUE LUNA ASSEMBLAGES

USES HIS FRIENDS' PUBIC HAIR

Enrique Luna specialises in mixed materials assemblages. 'Found objects', intimate body casts, clay, metal, wood, glass, paint and PUBIC HAIR are culled from himself and friends and transformed into statements of extraordinary sensuality. Both humor and violence lurk beneath the surface of his chosen juxtapositions.

SCANDAL IN CONNECTICUT

Last summer one of his pieces was removed from his Falls Village show prior to the opening and placed in a disused toilet. Those who had driven miles from NYC, alerted to this act of censorship, crowded the toilet to view this forbidden work. So potentially scandalous was the location that Luna is considering exhibiting his work in similar locations.

UNCUT SMOKESTACKS –
NO STRANGER TO CONTROVERSY

Luna is no stranger to controversy. A group show with fellow artists in his native Mexico City was raided by the police and closed down. Then there was the 'frisson' that ran through the Tucson first night of *L'Elisir d'Amore* with his design for the ARIZON OPERA COMPANY. When Dulcamara sailed on stage aboard a Mississippi paddleboat, the obviously 'uncut' smokestack caused opera glasses to quiver. Then there was his scandal of setting the opening scene of *Così Fan Tutte* in a bath house for Vermont's OPERA NORTH.

GERTRUDE STEIN AND GIANT BABIES

Luna has had many shows in his native Mexico City and is renowned for his opera and theatre design. He has a special relationship with New York's MEDICINE SHOW THEATRE

ENSEMBLE. He designed the world premiere of *The Domestic Baedeker of Gertrude Stein & Alice* for them. He has been awarded a NY State Council of the Arts grant to mount a production of *The Giant Baby* by Ionesco's mentor, surrealist Hungarian playwright, Tibor Déry and a show in the World Trade Center Gallery.

SPECIAL OPENING PARTY
Thursday 4th January at 7pm. Show runs thru to the 25th January, Wednesdays to Sundays, 12-6pm.

This was the press release I did in the NEW YORK NATIVE for Enrique's last show in January 1987. He had been feeling under the weather for several months and he collapsed at the opening night party. I took him to the St. Vincent's Hospital ER in the West Village. He was admitted and diagnosed with advanced AIDS. He had a T cell count of a mere 15 – the average healthy person has a count of 800 to 1,000. I nursed him for just over a year in New York and then took him home to Mexico City the following year. He died in March, 1988.

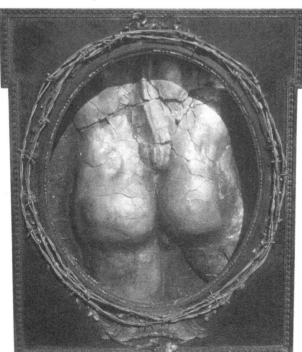

120.
El Amo Solar
November, 1987
24" x 36"
Assemblage: wood, barbed wire, clay, pubic hair.

Enrique Luna
May 16, 1946
Mexico City, Mexico
Set designer/ Artist.

110

TWO PLAGUE PORTRAITS

PERHAPS THE MOST EXTRAORDINARY patients were David Hampton (pictured below) and Charles Bradley – who really deserve that well worn cliché – you could not make this up.

David Hampton was the enigmatic confidence trickster whose life story formed the basis for John Guare's hit play *Six Degrees of Separation* in 1990. It later became a movie showcasing the talents of Will Smith – it was his first major role in film after a successful TV career as a rapper and the star of *The Fresh Prince of Bel-Air.*

David was born in Buffalo to comfortably-off middle-class mixed race parents. He moved to New York in 1981 when he

 was seventeen, intent on pursuing a career in the theatre. One night, with another teenage friend, they tried to get into Studio 54. They were turned away but returned an hour later having 'borrowed' a limo and posing as the young sons of Sidney Poitier and Gregory Peck. They were of course admitted by the celebrity conscious doorman. It was one of several roles he continued to play for the next nearly twenty years.

David would go to different fancy restaurants and tell the staff he was meeting his Dad. After ordering an expensive meal he would ask to use the house phone and then tell the staff that his father had been detained on business. The management would nearly always cover the tab.

He stole an address book from a man he had gone home with after being picked-up in a gay bar. It served as his entry into meeting some of Manhattan's glitziest celebrities, including Melanie Griffiths and Calvin Klein. His favourite *modus operandi* was to arrive at their doors, dishevelled, bloodied and saying he had been mugged and needed somewhere to clean-up and stay. Sometimes if his prior research indicated that his proposed victims had children of college age he would in addition pose as their son, or daughter's classmate.

It was said that he had tried to gain entry into Andy Warhol's studio, the Factory, but that Warhol sussed him out immediately. Wittily David would later explain that, "Andy was a con artist himself and one con artist can always spot another."

When Guare's play opened on Broadway to rave reviews David gate-crashed the opening night party and then hired a hot shot celebrity lawyer, Richard Golub, to sue the dramatist for appropriating his life – but the $100 million civil suit was thrown out. He appealed to no avail and hounded Guare – even with death threats but miraculously escaping prosecution.

David continued to dupe folks for money while attempting to pursue an acting career. At one audition he even claimed he was the actor who played himself as Poitier's son in *Six Degrees of Separation*.

One night in 1991 he tried to pick me up in the RAWHIDE bar in Chelsea. He told me he was an actor and understudying the lead in Guare's play! I was taken in and told him I was casting a new production of Carl Morse's play, *Minimum Wage*. I had by then directed the original productions of four of Carl's coruscating gay plays at La Mama and other Off-Off Broadway theatres during the 1990s. We were looking for someone to play Luis, the porter who gets a late night 'blow-job' in the deserted publishing company office the play is set in. I managed to extricate myself from this pushy young man but asked him to come and audition. He never turned up.

Years later in 1998, at the Peter Krueger Clinic, there he was sitting in my office as an intake patient. He told me that he had tested positive, was homeless and had no money. I did not remind him that we had met before and took him onto my caseload to sort out his needs.

He did not attend regularly, or keep his medical appointments, appearing only for moments of 'crisis intervention'. I discovered after a while that he was registered as a patient at several other HIV clinics, using a different name and therefore different Medicaid card and Social Security number.

In May 2003 I was visiting New York – having moved back to England to look after my mother when I retired from the hospital. An old co-worker told me David was an inpatient at Beth Israel and I learned later that he had subsequently died in July. This extraordinary young man who, people said, was the life and soul of many a party and had conned New York High Society, died alone. I do think he would have been thrilled to see he was important enough to deserve lengthy obituaries in the *New York Times*, *Guardian* and in *Playbill*, the Broadway theatre's programmes.

CHARLES BRADLEY was one of the nicest patients I ever looked after and he provided me with one of the most startling moments in my whole life.

It is late one evening in 2012 and I am back now in England watching a BBC music program – *Later with Jools Holland*. Jools started as the keyboard player with an 80s' pop band called *Squeeze* but is now renowned for his long running BBC2 show – where he brings together a hot mix of legendary and undiscovered artists in live and nearly always magical studio performances. He announces the name Charles Bradley (pictured below) and amazingly there is my 1990s' clinic patient strutting

in front of a six-piece soul band. Yes, I really did fall out of my chair as his raw raspy voice launched into a heavily-syncopated soul of a number called *The World Is Going Up In Flames.*

Flash backwards to some moment in 1996 and I am intaking a shy new patient who has just been discharged from the hospital after an almost fatal encounter with penicillin –a drug he is allergic to. He tells me he almost died and that he is seeing me because he tested positive while he was an inpatient. Over the following three years he met with me very regularly and I learned about his distressingly difficult and often tragic life.

Charles was born in Gainesville, Florida in 1948. His mother took flight when he was only 8 months and in early years was raised there by his grandmother. He never met his father. When he was eight his mother returned and took him to live with her in Bushwick, Brooklyn, with his older brother, Joseph. It was not a harmonious reunion. Charles often ran away from home living on the streets, begging by day and sleeping on the subway at night – sometimes even selling himself to predatory men to buy food. He told me that his mother scared him and that she would sometimes beat him and tell him that she wished he had never been born. "I was always in the wrong and could never do right by her."

When he was 17 he got a job in Maine and left home for good. For nearly ten years he worked in the kitchens of a mental hospital, progressing from being a dish washer to cooking. During this time he started entertaining his co-workers and friends with James Brown impersonations. He had never forgotten being taken by his sister to the Apollo in Harlem to see the legendary singer when he was a young teenager. Then Charles trekked across country to California and for the next twenty years survived by cooking in hospital canteens, doing odd jobs and occasionally earning extra money with his tribute act. In late 1994 his mother asked him to come back to Brooklyn to look after her as she was sick.

It was soon after this he arrived at the clinic after his discharge from the hospital. This was preceded by another tragedy – the murder of his beloved brother, Joseph, by one of his own nephews. Charles was profoundly shocked by this and I realised much later such traumas informed the lyrics of many of his songs. One song, *No Time for Dreaming*, on his second album *Victim of Love*, is a direct, harrowing memory of his brother's murder.

One day he invited a group of us from the clinic to come and see his James Brown tribute act. John Webber, the physician's assistant, whom he saw for his medical treatment, drove us to this rundown bar by the waterfront in Brooklyn. It was a revelation.

Despite using a pre-recorded backing tape, this was a vocal

performance made of exactly the same stuff as the man he was imitating. I could hardly believe this was the gentle and shy Charles I knew. Here was a voice of remarkable power and rawness – tough and terrifically dense, sometimes building to a scream that felt utterly primal and seemed to be coming not just from his lungs but from a deeply pained soul. It would be a real understatement to say we were all knocked sideways and devastated by his talent.

Soon after this I retired and came back to England. Charles gave me a tape of his act. He was one of the patients I had got close to. I kept in touch with him by phone and used to meet up for a Chinese meal with him at the restaurant by the hospital when I visited New York – he would never let me pay.

He had told me that he had met a record company producer but I had no idea of the extent of his late celebrity. Seeing him on the BBC TV show was my first premonition of this and it was confirmed when I found he was appearing at Glastonbury – the most prestigious of music festivals. He made three very well received albums and did several world tours as well as a punishing schedule of appearances in the States, Mexico and Canada.

Six years of this late in life fame came to an abrupt and sad close when in 2016 he was diagnosed with liver cancer. In September 2017 he died – he was 68.

His amazing life story and talent were celebrated in obituaries throughout the world including the *New York Times* and the *Guardian*. There were feature length articles in *Rolling Stone* and the *New Yorker*. He had even been nominated for an Emmy for a show he did on CBS.

I often wondered how he dealt with the business side of being a success, for Charles was semi-illiterate. He had needed help to complete all the paperwork to secure his Medicaid and benefits when he first came to me. I remember him saying to me when this late success beckoned that he wished I could be his manager!

I do know that for someone who had hobnobbed with John Lennon in a gay bar on the New York waterfront because it had the best retro blues and soul jukebox – and spent two weeks covering a young and not yet famous David Bowie for JEREMY magazine – for me, Charles was right up there in that pantheon. ■

attitude

THE BEST SELLING GAY MAGAZINE

LONG BEFORE OUR WORLD OF PRIDE AND THE PINK POUND

TIM HUGHES reflects on what it was like to be gay when it was illegal.

WHEN I WALK AROUND Manchester's gay village, or watch the Gay Pride March take four hours to pass me by on Fifth Avenue in New York, my mind often carries me back to far-off, very different, times.

As a teenager growing up in the grey, dreary and prejudiced post-war Britain of the 1950s, to be 'gay' – a word not yet fully imported from the USA – was not always exactly a fun thing.

To be 'queer', or a 'pouf', was definitely dangerous, as any kind of overt homosexual behaviour was deemed criminal and liable to prosecution. There were draconian prison sentences of up to ten years for the act of sodomy – a word that had replaced the original term of 'buggery'. There were heavy fines, and even prison sentences for the offence of 'public

> ## "The police forces in the UK routinely used cute young cadets to entrap unsuspecting 'cottagers'..."

indecency' – that is if you were caught with your pants down in a public toilet, or 'cruising' in a park.

The police forces in the UK routinely used cute young cadets to entrap unsuspecting 'cottagers' and a court appearance reported in your local paper destroyed many a career and marriage. The Sunday tabloids such as the *News of the World*, would crucify celebrities, or members of the establishment, with salacious front page exposure.

The most infamous case was in 1954 and concerned Lord Montagu – a peer of the realm and his two weekend guests, who were imprisoned for alleged 'indecent activities' with two young National Service members of the Royal Air Force at his Beaulieu Estate in Hampshire. This sensational case caused such a backlash among liberal sections of the establishment that it became the impetus for the formation of the parliamentary Wolfenden Committee Report in 1957. Its recommendations resulted ten years later in partial decriminalization for homosex.

Montagu revived his reputation by opening his world famous National Vintage Car museum at Beaulieu. He also earned an important place in LGBTQ history despite denying publicly that he was queer. And his name entered the language as a saucy synonym for anal intercourse – as in 'to Monty' someone.

Yet despite all these dire deterrents clandestine gaiety flourished. Public toilets were ubiquitous throughout the land and unless you lived in London, or one of the other larger cities with queer-friendly pubs, or a few very private members' drinking clubs, 'cottaging' was the only game in town.

'Trolling' (long before its unpleasant internet connotations), later overtaken by 'cruising' (another American gay slang import) – in parks and open spaces was the other popular way of meeting fellow travellers.

In the early 1960s, London's *Evening Standard* newspaper caused hilarity in the gay community with its exposé of 'the twilight world of Hampstead Heath – London's hidden problem'.

"...despite all these dire deterrents clandestine gaiety flourished. Public toilets were unbiquitous throughout the land..."

This series of prurient articles ensured lasting fame for the capital's premier cruising area.

There was a flourishing commercial side to gay sex. The eponymous 'Dilly Boys' plied their trade underneath the arches where Regent Street enters Piccadilly Circus, and in the pubs of enjoining Soho.

A rent boy apprenticeship was very often the only pathway for provincial working-class teenage lads' entry into our secretive gay world. With a complete absence of gay books, or any type of helpful media, it was a hit-or-miss experience for young people to find their way into any level of this underground outlaw society.

The somewhat then strait-laced BBC offered us the occasional

camp jesters like Kenneth Williams and Frankie Howerd. Beloved equally by a hetero audience, they never the less led unhappy private lives and were not accepted in the same way as today's 'out' gay celebrities are and were definitely not role models.

Drag queens were popular entertainers in ordinary pubs and some working men's clubs. Danny La Rue was the only rising cross-dressing cross-over star, but any inkling of the trans experience was confined to the sensational sex-change memoirs serialised in those same Sunday tabloids.

April Ashley (pictured above), a former Merchant Navy seaman from Liverpool who rose to the heights of London celebrity as a *Vogue* model, marrying a peer's son and opening a swanky restaurant, was the brand leader.

I myself was extremely lucky when I stumbled into 'the life' via an evening's cottage encounter as a teenager. This led to a series of non-predatory mentoring friendships with extraordinary older gay men. Some of them were celebrated in artistic circles. Several lived discreetly in relative privacy in loving partnerships without the current benefit of an undreamed-of civil partnership, or same-sex marriage. All the more special when it was almost unheard of for two men to share a flat without courting suspicion.

My new queer family showed me, by example, the holistic worth of a gay life – despite the then prevailing homophobia of a distinctly non-gay friendly outside world. But for many teens, I imagine, it must have been a life of absolute misery. ■

ATTITUDE MAGAZINE, 2021

Ingram Content Group UK Ltd.
Milton Keynes UK
UKHW020943200423
420482UK00003B/5